Locomotive Testing on Britain's Railways 1901-1968

A non-technical overview

Dave Peel

Kestrel Railway Books
PO Box 269
SOUTHAMPTON
SO30 4XR

www.kestrelrailwaybooks.co.uk

Printed by The Amadeus Press

ISBN 978-1-905505-31-9

Front cover: *Rugby Locomotive Testing Station opened on 19th October 1948 amid much publicity, and invited guests were treated to the spectacle of ex-LNER A4 4-6-2 60007 "Sir Nigel Gresley" running on the new machinery. This was not an engine test as such, just a demonstration for those present, but the locomotive chosen (named after the instigator of this national project) was most appropriate. Note the absence of the usual tender, measured quantities of coal and water being supplied via the adjustable "firing platform" behind the cab. (National Railway Museum/SSPL)*

Back cover, top: *Few non-BR locos were tested using a BR dynamometer car, but here a 500hp 0-8-0 diesel shunter destined for Peru has the former NER car attached at the head of a short freight, possibly on the Yeadon branch from Guiseley. The loco also worked Leeds-Lancaster goods turns during its spell of testing (between 2nd and 10th October 1951) and these were the last logged runs of the old NER car before withdrawal. The 0-8-0 sported blue and yellow livery, the colours of Leeds Rugby League Club – the Managing Director of Hunslet Engine Co was a keen supporter! (Collection RN Redman)*

Back cover, bottom: *Only two steam engines were ever coupled in earnest ahead of the 1961 WR car, one of which was 5056 "Earl of Powis" seen between Reading and Slough in July of that year. However, it is not the locomotive's performance that is being recorded, but the movement of its Automatic Train Control shoe, as it passes at speed over the ATC ramps fitted between the tracks at ground level. (National Railway Museum/SSPL)*

Contents

Acknowledgements

Personal thanks are due to the following for their assistance:

Alan Rimmer (Derby Testing Centre), Ron Pocklington (Rugby Testing Station), Peter Howe (Darlington Testing Centre), Doug Stagg (Swindon Test Plant), Pat Webb (Derby Testing Centre) and TD Allen Civil (WR Dynamometer Car).

Thanks also to the staff at the National Railway Museum, York; the British Library; the National Archive (Kew); the "Steam" Museum (Swindon); and the Great Western Trust (Didcot).

Photographers are individually credited. While every effort has been made to ensure that the attributions are accurate, if this is not the case, the author would welcome contact from the true copyright holder via the Publisher.

Bibliography

Major sources held at the National Railway Museum:

Test/Dyna/1A	LMS No 1 dynamometer car + log
Test/Dyna/2	LMS No 2 dynamometer car + log
Test/Dyna/3A	LMS No 3 dynamometer car + drawings
Test/Dyna/4A	LMS Test Train + Mobile Test Unit logs
Test/Dyna/5, 6	NER/LNER dynamometer cars; details
Test/Dyna/7A, B, C	LMS No 2 dynamometer car + log + runs with MTU No 2
Test/Dyna/8A-E	LMS No 3 dynamometer car + log
Test/Dyna/9	NER dynamometer car + log
Test/Dyna/10	LNER dynamometer car + log
Test/Dyna/11	GWR dynamometer car + log
Test/Dyna/12A, B	WR dynamometer car + log
Test/Test/2	Locomotive Testing Committee
Test/Test/5	Swindon Research Department Papers
Test/Test/6A-F	Swindon Research Department Papers

Testing Times at Derby by Alan Rimmer (Oakwood Press)
The Western Region Dynamometer Car by TD Allen Civil (published by the author)
History of the L&Y/LMS No 1 Dynamometer Car by Brian Radford (The Princess Royal Class Locomotive Trust)

In addition, many issues of periodicals with relevant articles have been consulted.

Abbreviations

ATC	Automatic Train Control
AWS	Automatic Warning System
NCB	National Coal Board
WD	War Department

Railway Companies:

CR	Caledonian Railway
ECJS	East Coast Joint Stock
GNR	Great Northern Railway
GWR	Great Western Railway
G&SWR	Glasgow & South Western Railway
LBSCR	London Brighton & South Coast Railway
LMS	London Midland & Scottish Railway
LNER	London & North Eastern Railway
LNWR	London North Western Railway
L&YR	Lancashire & Yorkshire Railway
NBR	North British Railway
NER	North Eastern Railway
S&DJR	Somerset and Dorset Joint Railway

Introduction

Although the first two words in the book's title might seem self-explanatory, both require some further explanation in this context.

Firstly, despite the steam locomotive occupying the major part of the story contained in these pages, other forms of motive power also appear. Clearly, the diesel engine makes its presence felt on BR, and does so with electric, hydraulic and mechanical transmission systems. Most of the first generation of main line diesel locomotives received the same form of on-the-road testing as did their steam counterparts, and there was even some dynamometer car testing involving small shunting engines and power cars of diesel multiple units. Gas turbines get an honourable mention, though only two (of three) had their performance recorded by a dynamometer car. In the later years, main line electric locomotives increased rapidly in number, and they too came under scrutiny. In this case, the tests primarily involved component parts (pantographs, bogies, springing, traction motors, etc) rather than the locomotive performance overall, and these tests pointed the way for the future use of test vehicles beyond the time-frame considered here.

Secondly the word "Testing" covers a multitude of possible procedures. Traditionally, it had grown to mean the measurement of how much weight an engine could pull, at what speed and at what cost in terms of coal and water. These are the things that the early dynamometer cars (specialised vehicles containing the scientific instruments) were designed to measure, and with increasing accuracy and sophistication, the later cars as well. This data could be used to compare, for example, an old type of engine with a new design from the same company, or to contrast two types with similar dimensions belonging to different railways. Alternatively, test results could be used to analyse differences in performance between engines of the same class, but fitted with different pieces of equipment. Yet again, an engine might be driven to its limit to establish what its maximum power output was, and hence to discover how much it had in reserve to make gains on daily schedules if necessary.

Most of the above testing was carried out on-the-road, with the dynamometer car coupled to the engine followed by the test train itself. This was often much heavier and longer than a normal service train, and this sometimes caused operational difficulties. A different method of testing was therefore to use either the Swindon or Rugby stationary test plants. Here, all the data required could be read with the engine *in situ* "on the rollers", though even these tests were followed by additional on-the-road tests to confirm the findings if the results were considered sufficiently important.

The choice, in the title, of the years 1901-68, covers the heyday of locomotive testing from the advent of the first dynamometer car through to the end of BR's activities in this area. In 1948, BR inherited the three dynamometer cars from 1901 (GWR), 1906 (NER) and 1913 (L&YR) around which testing had revolved for decades, plus the revamped Swindon Test Plant. With Rugby soon to be opened, and replacements for two of the three old dynamometer cars already in the pipeline, the following years were to become the busiest and most interesting testing years of all. The majority of the detail therefore refers to these years, but is preceded by a selection of the work done in the past by each of the three old cars, as essential historical background to the BR period.

By the end of this time, locomotive testing, as such, had ceased and the "Test Cars" as they were now called, were centralised at Derby and were no longer under Regional control. The cars themselves were re-equipped to include the ability to measure the dynamic movement of the (diesel or electric) locomotive and particularly, the new rolling stock. This could involve measuring the rolling resistance of Freightliner wagons, the rough riding of bogies, or the measurement of pressure changes in tunnels when two trains pass at speed – "tests" far removed from those undertaken in earlier years. As these are not locomotive tests *per se*, only a few are included on later pages as examples of the work carried out by these vehicles in subsequent years.

The title's subsidiary wording, "A non-technical overview", should come as relief to those who have seen any of the bulletins issued by BR and available to the general public. These are highly-detailed reports, full of technical terms, calculations, and pages (and pages!) of graphs describing aspects of the engines' performance. Even the enthusiast press of the day concentrated their comments on the highlights of the test runs, when maximum effort was being produced, and furnished their accounts with logs of speeds, timings and power output. In this book, therefore, you will not find references to "pounds of coal burnt per drawbar horsepower-hour", but you will find a relatively complete listing of where and when dynamometer cars were in operation, what engine was under test, and mostly, some indication of the purpose of the test. The latter also applies to those locomotives tested "on the rollers" at Swindon or Rugby. Many of the illustrations have appeared in print before, but as they largely relate to events of 50 to 60 years ago, the author feels justified in giving them another airing. The vast majority of the information contained in the text has been drawn from the National Railway Museum at York (as have the photographs), and a bibliography of sources used in this work is included for those interested in locating further details.

Overall, it hoped that this book will act as a readable, understandable and informative source on this topic. Previously, the subject has been dealt with either in a piecemeal fashion or as a technical subject, or both. Here, then, is an attempt to set before the reader a more complete picture of what was happening nationwide, together with a little of the history behind it all. Enjoy!

Dave Peel
Wareham, January 2013

"Britannia" class 4-6-2 70005 "John Milton" heads north through Skipton to rejoin its test train after turning itself, the LMR No 1 car, MTU 2 and 3 and the coal van on the Shipley triangle. These tests were the only ones in which the MTUs were operated manually from within each unit, as the remote control gear was fitted in No 3 car only. January/February 1952. (Patrick Webb)

Chapter 1

An Outline of the Origins and Development of Locomotive Testing

These occurred surprisingly early. The first instrumented vehicle to measure the amount of work an engine was doing in hauling a train was designed by Isambard Kingdom Brunel and Charles Babbage for the GWR in 1839. This was superseded in 1857 by Daniel Gooch's "Measuring Van", built for the broad gauge but later converted to standard gauge. This was able to measure and record simultaneously, the pull of the locomotive, the distance covered and the passage of time. From these three values the work done, the power and the speed could all be calculated, and the Van was used up to 1899 and replaced in 1901. In addition, Gooch also invented a form of steam engine "indicator" which showed, diagrammatically, how steam pressure varied in the cylinders.

From the late Victorian period onwards the use of indicators became fairly common on railways throughout the world, and gradually, further dynamometer cars of a more sophisticated nature were acquired by many of the larger, or richer, railway companies. The method of employing these vehicles did not change for several decades however. Engines to be tested ran either on ordinary trains (possibly with increased loads) or on special trains as convenience dictated, with the dynamometer car coupled immediately behind the tender.

In the early 1880s engineers in Russia suggested that a test train should be so run that the locomotive had to work in the same steady conditions for long enough for the relevant readings to be taken, and then properly related to one another. This implied running at constant speed with a fixed setting of the valve gear, though it also implied use of very long lengths of level, or constantly graded track. These physical conditions existed readily in Russia, but rarely elsewhere! To overcome this limitation, and to enable testing to be carried out on lines with varying gradients, the next step forward was to place a second, assisting engine, behind the dynamometer car, that could apply extra power on steeper grades in order to keep the speed constant. As a further development, any assisting engine that was fitted with a counter-pressure braking system (effectively running the engine in reverse) could also apply enough braking force for tests to be carried out on moderately downhill sections as well.

This system of testing in constant controlled conditions using a "brake locomotive" was developed further in the early 1900s, again in Russia, by Dr GV Lomonosoff. These test trains were regarded as so important that they had priority over virtually all other traffic, equal in fact to the Czar's train! The technique was spread to Poland after the first world war by one of Lomonosoff's pupils, and as a direct consequence of these test results, every important steam engine in Russia and Poland carried, in the cab, a form of "passport" relevant to that class, detailing to the driver the most effective and efficient way to work the locomotive in all circumstances.

The use of brake locomotives was taken up in many European countries, and in Great Britain by the LNER. Here, T Robson adapted an old North Eastern Railway 4-6-0 as a counter-pressure engine to such good effect that its ability to absorb power was greater than its former power output! DR Carling was working under Robson at this time, and it was no surprise when Carling took this engine with him to Rugby when he became Superintending Engineer at the new Locomotive Testing Station in 1948.

The development of this test plant at Rugby is told in greater detail later, suffice it to say here that it had endured a long gestation period (from 1927) and had been a joint venture between the LNER and LMS with opening delayed until after nationalisation, and seven years after the death of its main instigator, Sir Nigel Gresley.

Immediately before the Second World War, the LMS had also adopted, and adapted, the concept of brake locomotives for testing purposes. On this railway, the dynamometer car was followed by one, two or three mobile brake units. These were coaches with electric traction motors in the bogies which were not used as motors, but as generators for rheostatic braking. With the aid of electronic control from the dynamometer car (a very advanced application for the time) these units could be used to maintain either constant speed or constant pull regardless of gradient, or to simulate the effects of additional loads. Unfortunately, due to the war, this system was not complete and operational until 1949, after which BR made extensive use of it, mainly for tests on the London Midland Region. (For further details of the LMS Mobile Test Plant, see Chapter 7 on page 39.)

The LNER had inherited a dynamometer car from the North Eastern Railway. This had been built in 1906 and was a close copy of the 1901 GWR car. In fact there was strong cooperation between these two companies in its production, the GWR even lending the vehicle (and some drawings) to the NER for the purpose. The L&YR was also an early user of dynamometer cars, John Aspinall producing the first in 1896 and George Hughes replacing it in 1913. This became LMS property in 1923 as LMS No 1 dynamometer car, No 2 being the former LNWR car from 1908 (later a Flange Force test car only) and No 3 was designed to run either solo or in conjunction with its Mobile Test Plant. Work on No 3 had commenced prior to 1939, but was suspended during hostilities, with completion in 1949.

The LNER had also begun building a replacement for the NER car before the war. This too was delayed, and did not enter service until 1952. The oldest car, the GWR vehicle of 1901, was finally replaced by BR (Western Region) in 1961. Interestingly, both the LMS and LNER replacement cars, and the Rugby Testing Station were all equipped with

Amsler recording tables and Amsler hydraulic dynamometers (the main, and most costly pieces of scientific equipment within the vehicle), all of which had been ordered in 1939 from Messrs Alfred Amsler Ltd of Schaffhausen, Switzerland. They were ready for dispatch in 1940, but clearly there was a problem with transport at this time and it was well after the war had ended before they were delivered.

However, prolonged periods of track occupation by test trains running at set speeds could be a serious embarrassment to the operating department of a busy railway and there were not many stretches of line, not just in Britain, on which such trains could be conveniently accommodated. Consideration of these circumstances led to other methods of testing, one of which has already been mentioned above, in passing.

This is the construction of a locomotive test plant, where the locomotive runs on a set of rollers inside a building. An expensive piece of extra equipment, but compact and one which can clearly be fitted out with all the usual dynamometer car instrumentation (and more besides) all of which can be updated and adapted for testing other forms of motive power if required. Worldwide, and relevant to the time-scale affecting British practice, plants had been established by the Pennsylvania Railroad at Altoona (opened 1906, closed 1955), at Vitry (near Paris, 1933-72 at least), at Grunevald (Berlin 1930-45) and at Swindon (1904-59). This

latter, the first in Europe, was of limited capacity and was, in its early days used mainly for running-in engines after attention in the works, thus saving much track occupation on the main lines. After rebuilding in 1936/7 with greatly increased capacity, this plant became a very useful testing tool, and post-1948 was a key element along with Rugby, in BR's static testing programme.

Even with two stationary test plant facilities, the problem of track occupation with test trains moving at set speeds did not go away. A further method of road testing was therefore devised and developed by the GWR and the Western Region of British Railways. This became known as the Controlled Road Testing system whereby a locomotive worked at a constant rate of steaming (and also of firing). The consequence of this was that as the gradients varied, so did the speed, just like a normally scheduled service train, which made this type of test train much more acceptable to the operating department, as it was much easier to fit it into the timetable. This method of testing, pioneered by Sam Ell, was equally applicable to diesel or electric traction, and was used by the Swindon team in the dynamometer car road tests of engines that had (or had not, in the case of diesels) previously been on the Swindon test plant. This approach was later adopted nationally by BR as its standard method of road testing for locomotives undergoing full "Performance and

LNER 3-cylinder P2 2-8-2 2001 "Cock of the North" sports a large indicator shelter while working trials between King's Cross and Grantham. The picture was taken at Grantham some time between 19th June and 11th July 1934.
(National Railway Museum/SSPL)

2

Efficiency" tests, whether or not preceded by static tests at Swindon or Rugby.

Thus BR had at its disposal two stationary plants, two methods of road testing (constant steaming, or constant speed) and, at any one time, three or four dynamometer cars. Although the Swindon and Rugby plants were not updated for testing all aspects of non-steam power, all three dynamometer cars inherited by BR were gradually replaced in 1949, 1952 and 1961 and these new, modernised cars outlasted the test plants by many years, Swindon closing in 1959 and Rugby making its very last tests in 1965.

However, as will be appreciated, the disposition of these testing facilities was not exactly central. Swindon was self-contained in that the test plant and the dynamometer car were in the same building, and the same staff tested the locomotives both "on the rollers" and via the dynamometer car. Indeed, this car was deliberately housed on the track adjacent to the plant so that it could be used as an office while static tests took place, the car's portable recorder being used in conjunction with the plant's permanent equipment for data collection. Additionally, virtually all the subsequent road tests (if these were necessary) were based on circuits to and from Swindon.

The Rugby Testing Station did not have its own allocated dynamometer car, the Derby staff undertaking all the road-testing of engines ex-Rugby, and of other tests besides. The test routes emanated from neither Rugby nor Derby, but utilised almost exclusively two routes out and back from Carlisle. These were either the Settle & Carlisle line south to Skipton (with engines and testing vehicles running forward to Shipley to turn on the triangle), or the G&SWR line north to Hurlford (Kilmarnock), with operations based on the former Midland depot at Durran Hill if heading south, or Kingmoor if going north.

From the evidence of the various dynamometer car logs in the later pages, these "Performance and Efficiency" tests on the routes mentioned above constituted only a small proportion of the work performed by these cars, which roamed far and wide. The Eastern Region car was not involved in follow-up work from either Swindon or Rugby, and pursued its own programme based on Darlington, the car being stored when not in use at the Stooperdale paintshop within the North Road Works complex.

This car, continuing LNER tradition, had its own staff of four Dynamometer Car Inspectors (plus an Attendant), whereas the LMR cars had a staff of six and the WR seven, though all drew extra staff from their respective Drawing Offices as necessary.

On the other hand, the former Southern Railway did not possess either a stationary test plant or a dynamometer car, and in BR days simply "hired in" whichever car was available. From a perusal of the relevant logs it will be seen that the SR employed cars from all three possessing regions at one time or another, on a variety of traction! The Scottish Region was in a similar position, with its needs being supplied by either the LMR or ER car, as required.

At the conclusion of any series of test runs, the dynamometer car staff compiled a written report on the test, for submission to higher authority. If these tests were of the important "Performance and Efficiency" type, the reports were sometimes published as bulletins available to the general public. A resume of each of these (the non-technical sections!) is included near the end of this book.

The Locomotive Testing Committee

Given the extensive facilities available to it, and the experienced staff to operate them, the newly-formed BR needed to organise these resources quickly and effectively in order to maximise their potential. To this end the British Transport Commission instructed the Railway Executive to set up, as one of its Mechanical Engineering Policy Committees, the Locomotive Testing Committee. This body first met in January 1948 with the remit that:

"This Committee will make recommendations for the use and distribution of existing Testing Equipment and will draw attention to new apparatus and methods as they become available. It will co-ordinate programmes of testing between the Regions, and make recommendations thereon."

In company days, requests for tests or trials had originated in two main ways, which continued to be the case when BR took over. One would be an approach from the Chief Mechanical Engineer for the purpose of studying the relation between locomotive design, and performance, the other would be initiated by another department, and could relate to train timings with various loads, or stopping distances etc. All were now received by the new Locomotive Testing Committee, which prioritised those accepted, and allocated specific tests to specific resources.

As one of its first tasks was to organise the Locomotive Interchange Trials, which were due to start on 19 April 1948, this Committee had to be quick off the mark. These trials, their preparation and their aftermath, took up the greater part of the year for all dynamometer car testing staff. It might be appropriate therefore for readers unfamiliar with this landmark event to adjourn to the next (short) section, for further information.

The Committee as originally constituted had only five members, one from each of the regions that covered the pre-1948 companies, plus DR Carling, Superintending Engineer of the (yet to be opened) Rugby Testing Station. Once this facility was open and in operation, by March 1949 the Committee was expanded and reconstituted under the Chairmanship of ES Cox, Railway Executive Officer (Design), and of course there were some changes in personnel over the years. From this time onwards the Committee's work was heavy and continuous for the next ten years or so. It also received relevant reports throughout the year on the progress of tests in hand, and issued updated reviews of the current status of tests for each Committee meeting, held every two months or so. This Committee defined the policy regarding the standards of analysis and the presentation of test results, particularly the publicly available bulletins.

The Southern Railway possessed neither test plant nor dynamometer car, but still conducted indicator tests when appropriate. Here, Urie N15 4-6-0 742 (later named "Camelot") rests at Eastleigh on 7th June 1924. On 2-cylinder engines it was not necessary to fit "wrap-around" shelters, there being no cylinders between the frames. (HC Casserley, courtesy Richard Casserley)

Locomotive Interchange Trials 1948. Royal Scot class 4-6-0 46154 "The Hussar" is at the buffer stops at Waterloo after arriving on the 12.37pm from Exeter on 18th June. The engine has an 8-wheeled tender from a War Department loco (lettered LMS) for extra water capacity as the SR had no troughs, and the WR dynamometer car W7 is behind this. (National Railway Museum/SSPL)

Chapter 2

The Locomotive Interchange Trials of 1948

On the Nationalisation of the railways on 1st January 1948, the newly-formed Railway Executive had the unenviable task of welding four very large systems into a single working unit. Moreover, the Executive member RA Riddles, and recent appointees Chief Officer (Locomotive Works) RC Bond and Executive Officer (Design) ES Cox were all from the LMS, and unless public relations were carefully handled, accusations of bias (in locomotive terms) would soon arise, as new steam engines were being planned and these men would be responsible for them.

A two-pronged drive towards what might become future practice was quickly initiated, with ES Cox formulating outline plans for a range of standard designs, and an extensive series of Interchange Trials being organised for the spring and summer. These trials would be on a national basis and would include five express passenger types, four mixed traffic types and five heavy goods classes. All three dynamometer cars would be simultaneously employed to record engine performance, and the routes would cover WR, SR, LMR, ER and ScR territories, with representative types from each former company all running on "foreign" lines. By and large, all engines would be driven by crews familiar with them, accompanied on the footplate by a member of the dynamometer car staff and a pilotman if the crew was not on home ground. The trains hauled would be normal service trains, running to their normal schedules, though the train formations would be made up to agreed loads. The tests were to begin in April and end in September, the express passenger category going first and the freight types last.

The engines chosen were not given any special preparation and were taken direct from service operations, all having run between 15,000 and 20,000 miles since their last general overhaul. In the absence of a Locomotive Inspector on the footplate, crews were at liberty to drive and fire in their own accustomed manner. Some very different ways of working an engine were soon apparent – some crews had, as their first aim, to run the train to time regardless of coal, water consumption, whereas others, aware that the dynamometer car behind the tender was measuring their fuel consumption, sought to prove their engine was the most

economical. All trains suffered from the lack of a clear run, the Euston – Carlisle line being beset at this time with repairs and track maintenance restrictions for instance, though the worst affected trials were those between Brent and Toton, where only 1 in 16 of the freight trials was run to booked time.

The staff involved generally enjoyed the testing however, and certainly the enthusiasts of the day did, with widespread publicity being given to what the general public saw as an open contest. "Winning" was not the object of the exercise for the Railway Executive! For them, this was principally a means of establishing the most desirable features to incorporate in the design of future steam locomotives. At the end of the trials there was the strong impression that no one class of engine had shown such superiority over all the others that would single it out as the one to be standardised, which left Riddles and Cox with a rather more difficult task than anticipated!

Nevertheless, 220 test runs were made by the three dynamometer cars, over a total distance of 34,850 miles. This was useful experience for the staff involved, as the 1950s would see extensive use of these vehicles (and their subsequent replacements) in tests of a far more controlled and scientific nature than these trials. These future runs would often involve confirmation follow-up tests of locomotives that had undergone rigorous maximum power tests on the Rugby or Swindon test plants – a far cry from keeping to time with normal service trains in 1948.

Over the years, much has been written concerning the Interchange Trials and it would be superfluous to add further detail here. The accompanying photographs give a flavour of those times, and the captions provide extra information where appropriate. The following pages outline the schedules to be undertaken on a weekly basis, and repay close examination.

BR had given itself much extra work in putting on these trials, but in doing so had shown straight away that it was prepared to bring itself to the public's attention in a positive and unbiased way. No accusations could justifiably be brought to bear that LMS influence in subsequent "Standard" designs was there without deserving to be.

Interchange Trials 1948: Weekly Programme (next two pages)

Details in italics are familiarisation runs on Monday to Thursday. Other details are of test runs on Tuesday to Friday with a dynamometer car.

Note 1: 60022 fails at Savernake on 27th April and is replaced by 60033
Note 2: 60033 fails at Andover on 31st May and is replaced by 60022
Note 3: 60022 fails at Salisbury on 9th June and is replaced by 60034
Note 4: 48400 (in poor condition) is replaced by 48189 for 1st/2nd July
Note 5: 6001 with a 2-row superheater, 6022 with a 4-row superheater.

Notes regarding the WD locos participating in the trials:
2-8-0   63169 was later renumbered 90490, 77000 was later renumbered 90101
2-10-0   73774 was later renumbered 90750, 73776 was later renumbered 90752.

Week Comm.	Ex-LMS No 1 car	Loco	Ex-LNER car	Loco	Ex GWR car	Loco
19 Apr	10am Euston – Carlisle 12.55pm Carlisle – Euston	46236	1.10pm King's Cross – Leeds 7.50am Leeds – King's Cross	60034 46162	1.30pm Paddington – Plymouth 8.30am Plymouth – Paddington	6018 *35019*
26 April	—	—	1.10pm King's Cross – Leeds 7.50am Leeds – King's Cross	46162 46236	1.30pm Paddington – Plymouth 8.30am Plymouth – Paddington	35019 *60022/60033* (Note1)
3 May	10am Euston – Carlisle 12.55pm Carlisle – Euston *do.*	46162 35017	1.10pm King's Cross – Leeds 7.50am Leeds – King's Cross	46236	1.30pm Paddington – Plymouth 8.30am Plymouth – Paddington	60033
10 May	10am Euston – Carlisle 12.55pm Carlisle – Euston	35017	*1.10pm King's Cross – Leeds* *7.50am Leeds – King's Cross*	6018	*1.30pm Paddington – Plymouth* *8.30am Plymouth – Paddington*	46236
17 May	*10am Euston – Carlisle* *12.55pm Carlisle – Euston*	60034	1.10pm King's Cross – Leeds 7.50am Leeds – King's Cross do.	6018 *35019*	1.30pm Paddington – Plymouth 8.30am Plymouth – Paddington *do.*	46236 46162
24 May	10am Euston – Carlisle 12.55pm Carlisle – Euston	60034	1.10pm King's Cross – Leeds 7.50am Leeds – King's Cross	35017	1.30pm Paddington – Plymouth 8.30am Plymouth – Paddington	46162
31 May	10.15am St Pancras – Manchester 1.50pm Manchester – St Pancras	45253	10am Marylebone – Manchester 8.25am Manchester – Marylebone	61163 34006	10.50am Waterloo – Exeter 12.37pm Exeter – Waterloo	35018 *60033/60022* (Note 2)
7 June	*10.15am St Pancras – Manchester* *1.50pm Manchester – St Pancras*	*61251*	10am Marylebone – Manchester 8.25am Manchester – Marylebone *do.*	34006 45253	10.50am Waterloo – Exeter 12.37pm Exeter – Waterloo *do.*	60022/60034 (Note 3) 46154
14 June	10.15am St Pancras – Manchester 1.50pm Manchester – St Pancras *do.*	61251 34005	10am Marylebone – Manchester 8.25am Manchester – Marylebone	45253 6990	10.50am Waterloo – Exeter 12.37pm Exeter – Waterloo *do.*	46154 46236
21 June	10.15am St Pancras – Manchester 1.50pm Manchester – St Pancras	34005	10am Marylebone – Manchester 8.25am Manchester – Marylebone	6990	10.50am Waterloo – Exeter 12.37pm Exeter – Waterloo	46236

Date	Route (1)	Loco	Route (2)	Loco	Route (3)	Loco
28 June	10.40am Brent – Toton / 9.30am Toton – Brent	48400 / 48189 (Note 4)	—	—	1.45pm Bristol – Plymouth / 1.35pm Plymouth – Bristol	6990
5 July	10.40am Brent – Toton / 9.30am Toton – Brent	90490	4pm Perth – Inverness / 8.20am Inverness – Perth	44973	do.	61251 / 61251
12 July	10.40am Brent – Toton / 9.30am Toton – Brent	90752	4pm Perth – Inverness / 8.20am Inverness – Perth	34004 / 34004	1.45pm Bristol – Plymouth / 1.35pm Plymouth – Bristol	45253 / 45253
19 July	10.40am Brent – Toton / 9.30am Toton – Brent	63789 / 2-8-0 63789	4pm Perth – Inverness / 8.20am Inverness – Perth	61292 / 61292	do.	34006 / 34006
26 July	7.30am Ferme Park – New England / 8.5am New England – Ferme Park	2-8-0 63773	11.20am Acton – Severn T Jct / 2.40pm Severn T Jct – Hanwell	48189 / 48189	9.45am Bristol – Eastleigh / 11.36am Eastleigh – Bristol	2-8-0 3803
9 Aug	7.30am Ferme Park – New England / 8.5am New England – Ferme Park	90750	11.20am Acton – Severn T Jct / 2.40pm Severn T Jct – Hanwell	3803	9.45am Bristol – Eastleigh / 11.36am Eastleigh – Bristol	90101
16 Aug	7.30am Ferme Park – New England / 8.5am New England – Ferme Park	48189 / 48189	11.20am Acton – Severn T Jct / 2.40pm Severn T Jct – Hanwell	90750	do.	63789 / 63789
23 Aug	7.30am Ferme Park – New England / 8.5am New England – Ferme Park	3803 / 3803	11.20am Acton – Severn T Jct / 2.40pm Severn T Jct – Hanwell	90101	9.45am Bristol – Eastleigh / 11.36am Eastleigh – Bristol	90750
30 Aug	7.30am Ferme Park – New England / 8.5am New England – Ferme Park	90490	11.20am Acton – Severn T Jct / 2.40pm Severn T Jct – Hanwell	63773 / 63773	9.45am Bristol – Eastleigh / 11.36am Eastleigh – Bristol	48189 / 48189
22 Nov	Additional		—		1.30pm Paddington – Plymouth / 8.30am Plymouth – Paddington	6001 (Note 5)
29 Nov	Tests		—		1.45pm Bristol – Plymouth / 1.35pm Plymouth – Bristol	6961
6 Dec	using		—		11.15am Acton – Severn T Jct / 8.40am Severn T Jct – Hanwell	2-8-0 3864
13 Dec	Welsh coal		—		1.30pm Paddington – Plymouth / 8.30am Plymouth – Paddington	6022 (Note 5)

West Country class 4-6-2 34004 "Yeovil" heads the 8.20am from Inverness at the summit of Druimuachdar pass, at 1,484ft the highest main line point in Britain, paired with an LMS tender (with water scoop) followed by the ER dynamometer car on 14th July 1948. (National Railway Museum/SSPL)

Green-liveried B1 class 4-6-0 61251 "Oliver Bury" passes the once familiar gas holders immediately outside St Pancras station, bringing in the 1.50pm from Manchester on 18th June 1948. Its own tender reads "British Railways" in full and the LMR No 1 dynamometer car is the first vehicle. (National Railway Museum/SSPL)

Chapter 3

The Swindon Test Plant

GWR use when in original condition, 1904-1936

This plant, the first in Europe, was installed at the instigation of GJ Churchward and opened in 1904. Basically it consisted of five sets of rollers (three of which were braked) each independently movable to fit precisely beneath an engine's wheels. These brakes absorbed the power of the engine, and any wheel arrangement the GWR possessed could be tested (tender engines only). Tenders had to be removed, as the engines were fired from a firing platform (adjustable in height) onto which known amounts of coal could be fed at suitable intervals, and an external water supply fed the boiler with measurable quantities of water. The locomotives were anchored at the rear by means of a horizontal drawbar, which measured the pull of the engine, and the strength of this drawbar was a limiting factor. Initially it had been planned to build no less than four of these plants, alongside each other within the works complex, the main purpose of which would be to "run-in" engines after overhaul. To this end, considerable mileages were being covered on main lines that did not really have the capacity for large numbers of "light engine" movements for locomotives fresh from the workshops.

Consequently, the first use of the one plant actually put in place was mainly directed towards this goal, though it soon became clear that running on fixed rollers did not accurately replicate conditions "on the road", and its usefulness for this purpose therefore declined. Additionally, the total output from the engine that could be absorbed by the testing machinery was only of the order of 500 horsepower, a figure that was soon proved to be inadequate as larger and more powerful designs were added to stock, resulting in the facility becoming under-used.

In the near total absence of official records from this period regarding the exact use of the plant, and which engines were either run-in or tested in some manner, very little is definitively known. Hence, the following list of engines having been on the test plant is almost entirely based on the photographic record, which is bound to be incomplete. Moreover, it is quite probable that some of the photos were of special events laid on for visiting dignitaries rather than genuine tests of locomotives.

(*Note:* If a single date is quoted, it should not be assumed that this was the only day this loco occupied the plant, nor if a range is quoted, that tests happened every day. This is true of all three of the following lists. Enough information is simply not available.)

Engines that appeared on the test plant when in original condition, 1904-1936

1904	July	0-6-0 2460, Dean Goods
1907		0-6-0 874, built 1873, withdrawn 1913 [1]
1908		0-4-0T "Siemens" [2]
1908		0-4-0ST 92 [2]
1905-12		4-4-2 190, rebuilt as 4-6-0 2990 (2 cylinder) in 1912
1905-13		4-6-0 175 *Viscount Churchill*, renumbered 2975 in 1913
1924	25th April	2-6-0 6395
1929	May	4-6-0 4074 *Caldicot Castle* [3]
1932		4-6-0 4009 *Shooting Star*
1934		4-6-0 4925 *Eynesham Hall* [4]
1935	31st July to 17th August	4-6-0 2931 *Arlington Court* (see photo on page 10)
1935/6		4-6-0 4078 *Pembroke Castle*
1936/7	June to February	Plant extensively rebuilt

Notes:
1   Coal test (?) with new (Sept 1904) boiler, unsuperheated.
2   Boiler comparison tests made under the personal supervision of GJ Churchward. 92 has a standard GW boiler, "Siemens" has a Brotan boiler built by Beyer Peacock for British Mannesman Tube Co (Landore).
3   Probably provided for visit of French railway officials to the works.
4   Possibly mechanical lubricator tests.

Saint class 4-6-0 2931 "Arlington Court" stands motionless on the original Swindon test plant in an apparently deserted "A" shop on 17th August 1935. The belt-driven machinery was replaced when rebuilding took place between June 1936 and February 1937. (Steam – Museum of the GWR, Swindon)

GWR use after rebuilding, 1937-1947

Due to the inbuilt deficiencies of the original equipment, the GWR drew up plans in the mid-1930s to replace the test plant with a thoroughly modern equivalent (though keeping it in the same position). This was to be fully capable of absorbing in excess of 2000hp and of carrying out all the testing functions performed at other European establishments such as Vitry (near Paris) and Grunevald (near Berlin). Initially, the old "home trainer" as it was affectionately known, was overhauled and reconditioned during 1935, and it is likely that 2931 was used to run-in the machinery. Although these measures cost the GWR £2,500 (Directors minute dated 31st October 1935), it soon became apparent that new, replacement equipment was necessary if the requisite power (or more) was to be absorbed, and the plant was therefore totally rebuilt between June 1936 and February 1937 at a further cost of £3,450 (minute dated 25th November 1937). Together with other small alterations, the entire renewal costs were £6,950 14s 9d to the end of 1937. This two-stage enhancement (which was kept very quiet by Swindon) proved to be both a big surprise and a disappointment to the LNER and LMS authorities, as they were jointly engaged in planning the provision of a national locomotive testing station and hoped to recruit the GWR in order to spread the cost of

development. Having already gone it alone, the GWR therefore rejected these proposals, which eventually came to fruition (in 1948) as the Rugby Testing Station. BR of course made full use of both facilities until the end of the 1950s.

With this modernised equipment, Swindon was now able to embark on a programme of scientific testing of locomotive performance. Under the direction of SO Ell, Swindon proceeded to specialise in, and develop fully, the method of testing at a constant steam rate. This technique, applied equally on the plant and in controlled road tests with the dynamometer car, later became the standard BR method. It involved the firing of coal at a specific rate per hour (sometimes by two firemen), with the engine's power output being absorbed either by the test plant machinery, or by test trains of suitable (and increasing) weight. Swindon also became skilled in the design of the "front end" (the way in which steam passes into and out of the cylinders and is exhausted through the chimney) and in the design of chimney proportions. BR was to make effective use of this expertise, soon after nationalisation.

Again, few records survive from this period. Only the years 1944-47 contribute anything in writing at the NRM, and even these might be incomplete. Reliance is once more placed largely on photographic evidence to create the list below, with the same proviso mentioned previously.

Engines that appeared on the test plant after rebuilding, pre-1948

c. 1937		4-6-0 "Castle" [1]
1938		4-6-0 4041 *Prince of Wales*, "Star" class
1938	5th July	4-6-0 5014 *Goodrich Castle* [2]
1942	6th June to 9th July	4-6-0 5043 *Earl of Mount Edgcumbe*
1944	24th March to 3rd April	4-6-0 6959 *Peatling Hall*
	19th June-9th, 13th November	4-6-0 6966 *Witchingham Hall*
	10th, 11th, 14th, 15th November	4-6-0 6939 *Calverley Hall*
1945		0-6-0 2222, "tune-up" of plant, prior to:
	21st to 24th August	4-6-0 1000 *County of Middlesex*, double chimney
	9th, 10th October	4-6-0 1002 *County of Berks*, single chimney
	11th October	4-6-0 5008 *Raglan Castle*
1946/7		4-6-0 1007 *County of Brecknock* [3]
1947	5th, 7th March	4-6-0 4905 *Barton Hall*, plus road test with dynamometer car
		4-6-0 5056 *Earl of Powis*, plus road test with dynamometer car
	11th to 16th December	4-6-0 5049 *Earl of Plymouth*

Notes:
1 An unidentified loco underwent a partial test after the modification of plant, but before the removal of the original cab-drawbar dynamometer.
2 Provided for the visit of HRH Duke of Gloucester when also opening Swindon's new Town Hall.
3 Positioned (un-named) for publicity photo in Swindon Works booklet.

In January/February 1955, BR's sole 8P 71000 "Duke of Gloucester" was the first engine to use the modified plant. The WR dynamometer car W7 occupies its usual position on the adjacent road. Note the different appearance of the modern machinery and the larger chimney exhaust cowl compared with the previous photograph. (Author's Collection)

BR use, 1948-1959

Perhaps surprisingly, the extant details at York only take the record up to January 1950. However this entire period is very much better covered by the popular (enthusiast) press, and BR themselves published bulletins on some of the tests. Together with an extensive programme of follow-up road tests with the dynamometer car, it is much easier to trace out a clearer picture of the engines tested at Swindon during these years. More photographs were also taken at this time, and the combined evidence (even if the official records are scant)

produces a list which, in the author's opinion, has a high probability of being accurate. This applies to the particular locos, and the chronology, though the specific dates during which engines were tested on the plant are not possible to determine precisely. One further modification took place in 1954, when a fourth pair of braked rollers was added (see photograph of 71000 on page 11). This installation, with the alterations to the pit and drainage, cost BR £2,000, payment being authorised on 5th October 1954. (It is intriguing that no 8-coupled steam engine, nor B-B or Bo-Bo diesel ever made use of it!)

Engines that appeared on the test plant in the BR period, 1948-1959

1948	19th to 23rd March	4-6-0 6022 *King Edward III*, plus road test with dynamometer car. Newly fitted with 4-row superheater – first "King" so treated. Tested again in December as part of Interchange Trials.
1949	18th to 21st January	4-6-0 5049 *Earl of Plymouth*, plus road test with dynamometer car
	23rd February, 7th to 26th April	4-6-0 5087 *Tintern Abbey*, plus road test with dynamometer car
	7th to 29th June	4-6-0 5098 *Clifford Castle*, plus road test with dynamometer car 5049/87/98 boiler efficiency tests with 4/2/3-row superheaters respectively
	1st September	4-6-0 5018 *St Mawes Castle*, run for the benefit of the Ian Allan Locospotters Club visit
	25th October to 11th November	2-6-0 46413 Ivatt 2MT, plus road test with dynamometer car
1949/50	29th November to 7th December and 29th December to 4th January	0-6-0 2579 Dean Goods
1950	11th to 29th June	2-6-0 46413 Ivatt 2MT, plus road test with dynamometer car, re-draughting plus boiler efficiency tests, comparison with 2579 (see photograph opposite)
	12th May	4-6-0 7006 *Lydford Castle*, provided for summer visit of the Institution of Engineers
1951	22nd February	4-6-0 7916 *Mobberley Hall*, plus road test with dynamometer car (Bulletin 1)
		2-6-0 43094 Ivatt 4MT, plus road test with dynamometer car (Bulletin 3)
	27th November	4-6-0 75006 BR 4MT, plus road test with dynamometer car (Bulletin 4)
1952	16th to 23rd March	4-6-0 7818 *Granville Manor*, re-draughting plus boiler efficiency tests –100% increase in steam production! (See photograph on page 14.)
1952/3		2-6-2 60845 ER V2 class, plus road test with dynamometer car (Bulletin 8). Due to a leaking regulator, locomotive left plant of its own accord, driverless and tenderless, and steamed out into the yard! (See photograph on page 14.)
1953		4-6-0 6001 *King Edward VII*, plus road test with dynamometer car, boiler efficiency tests, 4-row superheater, modified single blast-pipe
1953/4	23rd September	4-6-0 1000 *County of Middlesex*, plus road test with dynamometer car, double-chimney tests
1954		4-6-0 1009 *County of Carmarthen*, plus road test with dynamometer car, stovepipe double-chimney tests
1955	January/February	4-6-2 71000 *Duke of Gloucester*, plus road test with dynamometer car (Bulletin 15)
1955/6	30th September	4-6-0 7018 *Drysllwyn Castle*, plus road test with dynamometer car, double-chimney tests (first "Castle" so fitted)

THE SWINDON TEST PLANT

1956		4-6-0 5057 *Earl Waldegrave*, posed for Works publicity booklet photograph
		4-6-0 6002 *King William IV*, plus road test with dynamometer car, double-chimney tests (first "King" so fitted)
1957	16th June	0-6-0 15100 GWR diesel electric 350hp shunter, adhesion tests (?) – the first non-steam engine tested
	August	4-6-2 35025 *Brocklebank Line*, revised valve settings, rebuilt "Merchant Navy", road test was with 35020 *Bibby Line* in June 1956
1957/8	2nd November to 5th January	2-10-0 92178 BR 9F, plus road test with dynamometer car, double-chimney tests – the first 9F so fitted
1958	4th March	4-6-0 5005 *Manorbier Castle*
	September	0-6-0PT 3711, the only tank engine tested, and only because it was an oil burner
1959	15th March	0-6-0 D3102 BR standard diesel electric 400hp shunter, adhesion tests (?) – the last engine tested
1961		Plant dismantled by September to provide extra space for diesel locomotive construction

The technicians' side of the test plant, with Class 2 2-6-0 46413 undergoing its second series of tests. W7 was used as an office when testing was in progress; some of its equipment was portable and was simply moved a few feet across to the tables shown here facing the locomotive. The chalk-board kept everyone informed! 21st June 1950.
(Steam – Museum of the GWR, Swindon)

13

As can be seen from the list, the last years of its regular use provided three surprises. Two of these were examples of the only non-steam types to run on the plant, both diesel shunters and both, it is believed, the subject of adhesion tests. The third refers to the only tank engine to be tested in BR days, an 0-6-0PT converted to an oil burner, so presumably the efficiency of the burner was under investigation. The list also contains no fewer than eight members of the "Castle" class 4-6-0, so it is highly likely some of these were instances of a publicity nature, rather than a scientific test.

Eventually the plant became redundant (though 4003 *Lode Star* was stored on the plant for a few months in 1961) and was dismantled later in that year, after a useful life of 55 years, none more so than the period 1948-59.

The Swindon Diesel Test Plant

The Western Region of BR was the only one whose diesel engines were connected to hydraulic transmissions. For comprehensive testing of new or rebuilt diesel engines (with hydraulic or mechanical transmissions) Heenan & Froud Ltd of Worcester installed two dynamometers suitable for testing railcar engines at Swindon in 1961.

This firm had already supplied two other dynamometers for the testing of the higher-powered engines and transmissions of Type 4 locomotives built at, or maintained by, Swindon, in 1960. (Derby and Doncaster both installed new test houses for diesel electric types in 1964 and late-1965 respectively, and by this time diesel locomotives were not generally subjected to road-testing with dynamometer cars. On the LMR and ER the power units were simply run-in on a test bed, either by the manufacturer, or by BR workshops.)

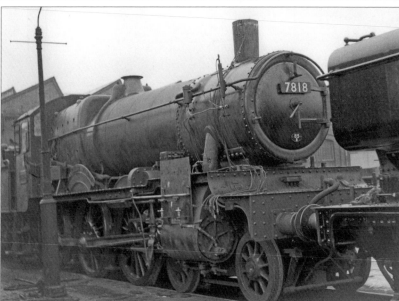

This page top: Perhaps surprisingly, ex-LNER V2 2-6-2 60845 went to Swindon for testing rather than to the plant at Rugby. Nevertheless Swindon did a good job in re-draughting the engine, confirmed by subsequent road tests. Although indoors, the V2 is fitted with a wooden indicator shelter, usually only seen on outdoor runs. 1st January 1953. (National Railway Museum/SSPL)

This page bottom: Between daily tests on the Plant, all engines were moved outside to discharge ash from the smokebox and rake out the fire. Here 7818 "Granville Manor" is in the midst of tests to improve its steaming capability, hence the unorthodox stovepipe chimney, and is seen outside "A" shop on 23rd March 1952. (National Railway Museum/SSPL)

Opposite page: The second of the rebuilt Merchant Navy class to emerge from Eastleigh Works, 35020 "Bibby Line" was chosen for road tests, and is seen here between Salisbury and Exeter in June 1956 with the WR car W7 (in carmine and cream livery) behind the tender. This is itself of interest, being the altered high-sided 6,000 gallon tender 3345, uniquely fitted to this rebuilt loco for the purposes of these tests only. (John Fry collection)

Chapter 4

GWR Dynamometer Car No 7

Built at Swindon in 1901, designed by GJ Churchward, and housed inside Swindon Works alongside the test plant, it was equipped with a spring dynamometer.

Pre-grouping use, significant runs only, 1901-1922

1901	23rd April	3005 Swindon-Taunton, engine test (first run of car)
1902	11th March	4-6-0 100 2-cyl, Swindon-Taunton, engine test (first Churchward express loco)
1903	21 July	4-6-0 98 2-cyl, Bristol-Newton Abbot, engine test (second Churchward express loco)
1903/4		Trials made on NER and GNR. Wilson Worsdell, Locomotive Superintendent of the NER, a personal friend of GJ Churchward, arranges to borrow his GWR dynamometer car for tests of a new NER 4-4-2 type. No 7 is attached to the 2.20pm departure from King's Cross to Scotland on 21st November 1903 behind GNR 4-4-2 251 (as far as Doncaster) and NER 4-4-2 532 to Newcastle. Trials continue until 3rd February 1904. NER subsequently builds a dynamometer car similar to No 7.
1904	4th February	4-cyl 4-4-2 102 *La France*, Paddington-Bristol, engine test
1904	13th April	2-cyl 4-6-0 171 *Albion*, Paddington-Bristol, engine test (third Churchward express loco)
1905	13th July	4-cyl 4-4-2 103 *President*, Laira-Newton Abbot, engine test
1909	14th to 16th November	On loan to LBSCR. Makes five runs between Victoria and Brighton with LBSCR locos 545, 40, 25 and 23, engine tests
1910	24th August	4-6-0 1471 LNWR "Experiment" class, Paddington-Exeter, engine test
1914-18	7th February 1914 to 31st May 1918	On loan to GNR recording engine tests on various routes from King's Cross to Doncaster, York and Lincoln
1922	16th May	Calibration tests with GWR/NER dynamometer cars from Peterborough to Boston and return
	22nd to 29th May	On loan to GNR for wagon resistance tests, Peterborough-Boston

Post-grouping use, significant runs only, 1923-1939

1924	14th to 26th March	4074 *Caldicot Castle*, Swindon-Plymouth, engine tests
1926	22nd July to 10th September	4074 *Caldicot Castle*, Paddington-Bristol, engine tests
1928	17th December	6009 *King Charles II*, Bristol-Paddington, engine test
1933	25th March	6001 *King Edward VII*, Stapleton Road-Wootton Bassett, speedometer trial
1936	4th March	Severn Tunnel pumping engine at Sudbrooke

Wartime use

| 1944 | 17th April | USA diesel electric 8121, Swansea-Newport, engine test |

Post-war GWR use, 1946/7

1946	10th, 14th April	5056 *Earl of Powis*, Reading-Maidenhead, high-speed test, multiple aspect ATC
1947	15th April to 4th September	4905 *Barton Hall*, Swindon-Stoke Gifford cylinder lubrication test for Anglo-Iranian Oil Company
1947 (last GWR use)	28th October	0-4-2T 5423, Swindon-Stoke Gifford, acceleration/braking test

Q: How many men does it take to run a Controlled Road Test? A: At least twenty! This is probably the end-of-testing group shot at Swindon in May 1951, the results being published as Bulletin 1. Note the indicator shelter at the front of the engine, 7916 "Mobberley Hall". (Author's collection)

British Railways use, 1948-1961

Car now numbered W7, later W7W.

1948		Car to Derby for calibration with LMS No 1 car, 25th/26th February. After this, the whole of the year's use was directed towards the Interchange Trials, commencing with 6018 *King Henry VI*, Paddington-Plymouth (20th April) through to 8F 2-8-0 48189 Eastleigh-Bristol (3rd September). Welsh steam coal tests began with 6001 *King Edward VII*, Paddington-Plymouth (23rd November) and finished with 6022 *King Edward III*, Plymouth-Paddington (17th December). (See photograph on page 4.)
1949	8th to 11th February	5049 *Earl of Plymouth*, Cardiff-Paddington and back (4-row superheater tests)
	1st to 3rd March	5087 *Tintern Abbey*, Cardiff-Paddington (2-row superheater tests)
	17th to 20th May	5098 *Clifford Castle*, Cardiff-Paddington (3-row superheater tests)
	21st to 25th November and 11th December	2MT 2-6-0 46413, Swindon-Bristol, steaming tests
1950	27th February to 17th March	111 *Viscount Churchill*, Swindon-Stoke Gifford, brake tests
	21st April	2500hp A1A-A1A 18000 gas turbine, Bristol-Swindon, performance and efficiency test
	27th June	18000 gas turbine, Paddington-Westbury and back, demonstration run
	21st to 25th August	2MT 2-6-0 46413, Stoke Gifford-Marston Sidings, constant steaming trials
	26th to 29th September	5049 *Earl of Plymouth*, Paddington-Plymouth
	10th to 13th October	6022 *King Edward III*, Paddington-Plymouth, comparative efficiency tests between 18000, 5049 and 6022
	27th November to 7th December	111 *Viscount Churchill*, Swindon-Stoke Gifford, brake test
1951	22nd to 31st May	7916 *Mobberley Hall*, Wantage Road-Filton, controlled road tests for Bulletin 1
	11th to 14th September	18000 gas turbine, Paddington-Plymouth, performance and efficiency tests
	24th September to 5th October	4MT 2-6-0 43094, Wantage Road-Filton, controlled road tests for Bulletin 3
1952	15th to 25th January	4MT 4-6-0 75006, Didcot-Stoke Gifford and back, controlled road tests
	20th to 21st February	4MT 4-6-0 75006, Swindon-Stoke Gifford-Didcot, controlled road tests for Bulletin 4
	28th April to 1st May	1750hp 1Co-Co1 10202 diesel electric, Waterloo-Exeter, performance and efficiency tests for Bulletin 9
	Four days in October	1750hp 1Co-Co1 10202 diesel electric, Exeter-Salisbury, performance and efficiency tests for Bulletin 9
1953	24th to 26th February and 3rd to 5th March	V2 2-6-2 60845, Reading-Bristol and back controlled road tests for Bulletin 8
	13th May	70025 *Western Star*, Cardiff-Paddington, special for International Railway Congress
	29th June to 23rd July	6001 *King Edward VII*, Reading-Stoke Gifford and back, controlled road tests
	1st September	6001 *King Edward VII*, Paddington-Bristol, 2hr "Bristolian" timing test
1954	12th to 22nd January	1000 *County of Middlesex*, Reading-Stoke Gifford and back, controlled road tests
	30th April	6003 *King George IV*, Paddington-Bristol, 1¾hr "Bristolian" timing test
	27th May	9F 2-10-0 92002, Swindon Works yard, full brake/tender hand brake tests
	10th to 11th June	70015 *Apollo*, Swindon-Stoke Gifford and back, brake tests with freight trains
	2nd to 19th November	1009 *County of Carmarthen*, Reading-Stoke Gifford and back, controlled road tests

1955	8th to 11th March	6013 *King Henry VIII*, Paddington-Plymouth, 4hr "Cornish Riviera" timing test
	15th to 29th April	71000 *Duke of Gloucester*, Swindon-Reading-Westbury and back, controlled road tests for Bulletin 15
	13th May	46237 *City of Bristol*, Paddington-Wolverhampton and back
	17th to 20th May	46237 *City of Bristol*, Paddington-Plymouth, 4hr "Cornish Riviera" timing test
	28th to 30th June and 1st July	2000hp 1Co-Co1 10203 diesel electric, Exeter-Salisbury, performance and efficiency tests for Bulletin 16
	4th to 7th July	2000hp 1Co-Co1 10203 diesel electric, Exeter-Waterloo, performance and efficiency tests for Bulletin 16
	9th December	70028 *Royal Star*, Swindon-Didcot, investigation into Milton accident
1956	28th to 31st May	6002 *King William IV*, Paddington-Plymouth, double chimney tests
	1st June	6002 *King William IV*, Paddington-Wolverhampton, double chimney tests
	12th to 22nd June	35020 *Bibby Line*, Exeter-Salisbury and back, controlled road tests for Bulletin 20
	25th to 28th June	35020 *Bibby Line*, Exeter-Waterloo and back, controlled road tests for Bulletin 20
	24th to 27th July	7018 *Drysllwyn Castle*, Paddington-Kingswear-Newton Abbot, double chimney tests
	14th to 24th August	7037 *Swindon*, Swindon-Stoke Gifford and back, vacuum trials
	28th to 31st August	70026 *Polar Star*, Swindon-Stoke Gifford and back, vacuum trials
	15th October to 14th December	4953 *Pitchford Hall*, brake tests, empty/loaded wagons
1957	21st January to 15th February	2-8-0 2865, Swindon-Stoke Gifford and back, vacuum trials and resistance tests
	5th March	7037 *Swindon*, Swindon-Stoke Gifford and back, Guard's brake tests
	18th, 19th and 25th, 26th June	4MT 4-6-0 75029 (double chimney), Bristol-Weymouth and back, controlled road tests
	11th to 21st November	6955 *Lydcott Hall*, ATC trials with fully-fitted freights
1958	28rd to 30th January and 4th to 7th February	9F 2-10-0 92178 (double chimney), Reading-Stoke Gifford and back, controlled road tests
	17th February	2000hp A1A-A1A D600 *Active*, Paddington-Bristol and back, demonstration run
	23rd April to 2nd May and 3rd to 6th June	D601 *Ark Royal*, Swindon-Stoke Gifford and back, brake and ATC tests, passenger stock, then freight
	15th May	D601 *Ark Royal*, Newton Abbot-Plymouth and back, starting tests, maximum load
	11th June	D601 *Ark Royal*, Newton Abbot-Plymouth and back, double-headed by a "Castle", "Hall" and "Manor" in turn
	11th July	D600 *Active*, Swindon-Stoke Gifford and back, brake tests, passenger stock
	10th August	2000hp B-B D800 *Sir Brian Robertson*, Swindon-Plymouth and back, performance and efficiency test
	26th, 28th August	2-8-0 48431, Avonmouth-Birmingham and back, Esso tank wagons test
	5 days in September	7037 *Swindon*, Swindon-Stoke Gifford and back, emergency braking tests
	2nd October (rehearsal) and 20th to 24th October	D801 *Vanguard*, Swindon-Stoke Gifford and back, performance and efficiency tests
	9th, 10th October	D801 *Vanguard*, Swindon-Bath-Didcot-Swindon, high-speed braking tests
	7th November	70028 *Royal Star*, Swindon-Bristol and back, drawgear test to reduce oscillations
1959-61		Although W7W remained in service until 1961, records for these years have not been located (if they still exist)

Use after withdrawal by BR

The car remained at Swindon for several years after coming out of use, being seen in the works yard in 1964, still apparently intact. It was eventually purchased by the preservation society operating the Totnes to Buckfastleigh line, where it remains to this day.

With substantial internal alterations (including the removal of all the remaining testing equipment) it was originally proposed that it become part of a "Victorian" train. Although this never really materialised, it is not suitable for carrying passengers, but is occasionally used at limited speed, usually for filming purposes.

Above: King class 4-6-0 6001 "King Edward VII" undergoing road testing between Reading and Stoke Gifford in the summer of 1953, with a long rake of empty carriage stock behind W7. The (very large) indicator shelter is prominent, complete with a tarpaulin for further protection! Being a four-cylinder engine, the outside cylinders were set further back than on the 2-cylinder 4-6-0s, hence the rearward extension of the shelter along much of the running plate. (Author's collection)

Below: The Brown-Boveri gas turbine A1A-A1A 18000 was given performance and efficiency tests between Plymouth and Paddington, and is seen here with a short 6-coach express (seven including the old dynamometer car). (National Railway Museum/SSPL)

Above: Between 6th and 8th February 1962, the Brush Co-Co "Falcon" was given maximum load tests on the Lickey incline south of Birmingham, including restarting a 20-coach load from milepost 55. By this time, the new WR dynamometer car was in operation to record the results. Hopefully the person in the white overalls will be able to see the guard's green flag! *(Brush Traction/TD Allen Civil Collection)*

Below: A busy scene inside WR dynamometer car DW150192 during the course of tests with "Falcon" on the Bristol main line in January 1962, most of the Swindon Testing Department being present. *(Brush Traction/Author's Collection)*

Chapter 5

WR Dynamometer Car No DW150192

First conceived in 1958, this was converted from a 63ft long (2nd class), wooden-bodied, corridor passenger coach of GWR origin, W796. The car was built to the requirements of RA Smeddle, Chief Mechanical and Electrical Engineer (Swindon) and the Research & Development (Rolling Stock) Office, at the Swindon Carriage & Wagon workshops, and painted in chocolate and cream livery. Completed in 1961, it owes much to the energy and enthusiasm of SO Ell and his testing team. The car had neither a spring nor a hydraulic dynamometer, but used electronic equipment built in-house and was therefore designed very much with diesel or electric motive power in mind. The design requirements were five-fold:

- To record all measurements taken during controlled road testing of steam or non-steam types
- To provide for the investigation of the internal working of diesel and electric locomotives
- To provide for the investigation of general problems associated with adhesion, braking, stressing of parts, vehicle riding, etc
- To provide for the widest application of modern electronic instrumentation
- To provide (as far as possible under mobile conditions) laboratory-standard facilities for all of the above.

When not in use, the car was stored in the C&W No 19 workshop at Swindon along with Track Testing Car W139.

1961	12th May	Inspected by the Duke of Edinburgh at the Marylebone Exhibition of rolling stock on the occasion of the Golden Jubilee of the Institution of Locomotive Engineers, not yet fully fitted out
	5th July	First public appearance. Swindon-Bristol and back, out via Bath, back via Badminton. Running-in, with SO Ell and invited R&D staff.
	11th July	5056 *Earl of Powis*, Reading-Slough, measure movement of ATC shoe on locomotive at moderate speeds
	16th and 23rd July	5056 *Earl of Powis*, Reading-Slough, high-speed tests over ATC ramps (94mph achieved)
	31st August	2200hp B-B D853 *Thruster*, Plymouth-Paddington and back examine overheating of axles
	20th, 21st September	2500hp 1Co-Co1 D40, Lickey incline, maximum load tests, 500 tons restarted and accelerated to 18mph
	5 days in October to December	D821 *Greyhound*, Athelney-Durston, tests of modernised ATC system on freight trains
	5 days in October to December	D821 *Greyhound*, Swindon-Stoke Gifford and back, stopping distance tests with 12-coach trains from 92mph max
1962	3rd and 17th January	D814 *Dragon*, Plymouth-Paddington, axlebox overheating tests. The test on 3rd January failed due to faults on both the locomotive and the dynamometer car, and was repeated on 17th January.
	23rd Jan to 2nd February	2800hp Co-Co D0280 *Falcon*, Didcot-Bristol and back, performance and efficiency tests at the request of the BTC and Brush, 100mph max speed, 600 ton max load, 20 staff involved!
	6th to 8th February	D0280 *Falcon*, Lickey incline, maximum load tests, 628 tons restarted from milepost 55, plus brake tests down incline (see photographs opposite)
	13th February	D0280 *Falcon*, Newton Abbot-Plymouth maximum load tests, 567 tons restarted on Dainton and Hemerdon banks
	29th March	1700hp B-B D7011, Swindon-Stoke Gifford and back, transmission shaft failure tests
	17th, 18th and 25th April	2700hp C-C D1000 *Western Enterprise*, Didcot-Bristol and back, controller settings tests

1962 continued	24th July to 2nd August	2750hp Co-Co D0260 *Lion*, Didcot-Bristol and back, performance and efficiency tests at the request of the BTC and the Birmingham Railway Carriage & Wagon Co, max load 567 tons. The test train on 25th July ran to Gloucester for inspection by the Commissioner of Australian Railways and the Chief Civil Engineer of Western Australian Railways.
	14th August	D0260 *Lion*, Swindon-Plymouth and back, maximum load tests – stalls on Dainton with 567 tons
	15th August	D0260 *Lion*, Lickey incline, max load tests, 635 tons restarted from milepost 55
	28th to 30th August	D0260 *Lion*, Didcot-Bristol and back, riding tests. A representative from Malayan Railways attended these tests. Swindon-Taunton and back, 30th August.
	6th, 7th and 10th December	D821 *Greyhound*, Athelney-Durston, braking tests with freight vehicles. DW150192 incurred damage to its buffing and drawgear on the last test due to severe impacts with the freight vehicles.
1963	5th to 13th February	2750hp Co-Co D1500, Didcot-Bristol and back, performance and efficiency tests, 103mph max speed, 571 tons max load used (17 coaches)
	19th February	D1500, Swindon-Plymouth and back, maximum load tests on South Devon banks, all starts OK
	20th February	D1500, Lickey incline, maximum load tests, 637 tons restarted from milepost 55 to 17½ mph
	13 days in March to May	0-6-0ST 3883, Yarnton-Kingham, tests of Hunslet gas-producer firebox system as fitted to an "Austerity" type locomotive in conjunction with the arrangement of blastpipe and chimney. Gross load: 369 tons. The boiler eventually produced 12,000lb steam/hr (6,000 as received). The test was commissioned by the Hunslet Engine Co, Leeds. 10th May 1963 was the last date on which a steam engine was tested in this country. (See photograph on page 24.)
	Various days in June to August	D7082, Swindon-Bristol or Cardiff and back, tests to evaluate gearbox failures (tests repeated 12th/13th and 24th/25th September). A BBC TV schools unit travelled from Swindon to Patchway to film inside the dynamometer car on 9th August.
	27th to 30th August	1750hp Co-Co D6860, Swindon-Bristol and back, controller settings tests
	3rd to 6th September	D6860, Lickey incline, maximum load tests, 505 tons restarted from milepost 55, also maximum freight loads, Rogerston-Ebbw Vale
	14th to 18th October	D6860, Swindon-Bristol and back, tests with prototype inter-Regional BR AWS
	23rd October	D1039 *Western King*, Swindon-Cardiff and back to investigate engine crankshaft failures
	6th, 7th and 26th November	D7082, Swindon-Cardiff and back, tests with various damping devices
1964	22nd, 23rd January	D1008 *Western Harrier*, Swindon-Bristol and back, 5-coach train to run up to 100mph with track testing car W139 in formation. Also test to investigate over-speed trip operation. These tests were at the instigation of the Chief Civil Engineer.
	19th February to 3rd March	1550hp Bo-Bo D6553, Swindon-Bristol-Didcot-Swindon to investigate riding of freightliner wagons
	8th to 11th June and 15th, 16th June	D1029 *Western Legionnaire*, (route as above), performance and efficiency tests, 102mph max speed (7-15 coaches, 238-501 tons)
	17th June	D1029 *Western Legionnaire*, Lickey incline, maximum load tests, 604 tons restarted from milepost 55 to 13mph. Due to a transmission failure, the 18-coach train was worked between Bromsgrove and Cheltenham on one engine. D1029 then successfully restarted a train of 11 coaches on the 1 in 58 of Sapperton bank without slipping, still on only one engine!

	29th June	D1029 *Western Legionnaire*, Swindon-Plymouth and back, maximum load tests on South Devon banks (15 coaches), restarts on Dainton at second attempt
	15th to 24th September	D6826, Swindon-Bristol-Didcot-Swindon, riding/braking tests of Cartic 4 wagons
	7 days in December	650hp 0-6-0 D9517, Swindon-Stoke Gifford and back, full performance and efficiency tests, maximum load 11 coaches, 367 tons
	17th, 18th December	D9517, Swindon Town-Rushey Platt, low speed tests 4-10mph with 308-561 tons
1965	12th, 13th January	D9517, Lickey incline, maximum load tests, 337 tons restarted from milepost 55 to 7mph
	9 days in April	D9517, Swindon-Stoke Gifford and back, brake-block tests with a load between 1 and 12 coaches
	16th, 17th June	D841 *Roebuck*, Bristol-Plymouth passenger train, then Tavistock-Bristol freight, reliability test of NBL/MAN diesel engine

The records held at the National Railway Museum end here. Isolated subsequent uses of the car now follow.

1966	9th March	D1050 *Western Ruler*, Lickey incline, 8 vehicles (one engine only?)
	May	D1613, Taunton-Bristol, brake tests with coaches
	May	D1613, Cheltenham-Honeybourne, brake tests with freight wagons
1967		All testing work centralised at the newly-opened Railway Technical Centre, Derby. All dynamometer cars and staff now located there.
1968	30th January to 14th February	D6700, Doncaster-Lincoln/Peterborough and back, hauling and propelling tests for high-speed push/pull services
	15th to 22nd February	D1938, Doncaster-Peterborough/Sandy and back, hauling and propelling tests and inner buffing loads on curves investigated
	7th June to 8th November	D61, Derby-Crewe-Carnforth-Leeds-Sheffield-Derby, tests on Mk II 1st class coaches: wheel balancing, heating, ventilation and air conditioning
	27th, 28th November	DW150192/REP 3006/3TC, Stewarts Lane-Brockenhurst or Eastleigh, riding tests on new Bournemouth stock
1969	4th to 8th August	EE Type 3, Cargo Fleet-Consett, ride tests with molten steel "Torpedo" wagons
1970	18th December	To Swindon Works for overhaul, dual brake fitted, repainted from chocolate and cream to blue and red, and renamed Test Car 4

Use after withdrawal by BR

As Test Car 4, this vehicle continued in service throughout the 1970s, but made its last run in June 1981. Damage was sustained to its buffing gear at the end of a test, and the car was transferred to sidings at the Railway Technical Centre and condemned there. After the removal of usable equipment, the car was put up for sale. Initially sold to a Midlands scrap dealer, it was resold to a private buyer, and removed by road from Derby to the Foxfield Railway (near Stoke-on-Trent) in 1983. Here, in red/blue Test Car livery, it was in use as a coach/buffet car/party car (equipped with 18 seats) during 1983/4. The vehicle was repainted in WR colours during 1984 in preparation for an exhibition at Swindon Works in 1985 as part of the sesquicentenary celebrations of the GWR, but in the event, this exhibition was cancelled as closure of these famous works was announced for 1986, and co-operation was withdrawn!

Around 1989, the car was acquired privately on behalf of the 71000 *Duke of Gloucester* Steam Locomotive Trust Limited, taken to BR's Wolverton Carriage Works, restored to full chocolate and cream livery and rechristened DW 150192. The steel side-panelling was also replaced, and the car was then transferred to Didcot (where 71000 was kept at the time). The original intention was to restore the car in order to test 71000, and some equipment was installed, but also some was missing. It did however accompany 71000 on several runs as an additional (saloon) coach during 1990/1. Being wooden-bodied, it could not carry fare-paying passengers on the main line, so when its Network Rail registration ran out the car was taken out of use. It remained at Didcot until the late 1990s, after which it was again sold and removed to the West Coast Railway site at Carnforth. Here it remains, still in private hands, in open store and exposed to the elements, but with an uncertain future.

Above: The very last steam engine to be tested with a dynamometer car wasn't even a BR loco! It was a Hunslet 0-6-0ST owned by the NCB and was experimentally fitted with a gas-producer firebox and altered draughting arrangements for evaluation during the Spring of 1963. The locomotive is seen here taking water in Yarnton yard on the Oxford-Worcester line with the then (relatively) new WR dynamometer car, DW150192, doing the honours. (TD Allen Civil collection)

Below: The last time a steam locomotive was indicated was in 1958 (see page 67). Here, A1 class 4-6-2 60136 "Alcazar" leaves Doncaster on the 8.32am to King's Cross on 2ⁿᵈ May. Working behind the shelter at 98mph was apparently quite exacting! (Author's collection)

Chapter 6

Rugby Locomotive Testing Station

The concept of a national locomotive testing facility was first proposed by HN Gresley in 1927. He was at that time the Chief Mechanical Engineer (CME) of the London & North Eastern Railway and also President of the Institution of Locomotive Engineers, and it was in this capacity that he first suggested the idea in his presidential address to the Institution on 29th September 1927. The following year a committee from the four main companies was formed to examine the possibility, but due to the economic slump, the report was shelved until 1934, and after Gresley had reiterated his interest, a new committee revived the proposal. However, by 1936 the Southern Railway had decided that its future lay in third-rail electrification and the Great Western was in the process of modernising its own test plant. Hence the LNER, together with the London, Midland & Scottish Railway announced that they would proceed jointly with the construction of a testing facility. To this end, in 1937, two committees were formed, one comprising directors and chief officers of both railways, and a second management committee consisting of Sir Nigel Gresley (knighted the previous year) and WA Stanier, CME of the LMS. A Superintending Engineer RC Bond was appointed to control all the activities at the embryonic station and to be directly answerable to the two CMEs.

The management committee, in collaboration with the firm of Heenan & Froude Ltd of Worcester, was responsible for the design of the testing station and its complete specification, and as Gresley had sent one of his 2-8-2 engines, *Cock o' the North*, to the Vitry test plant in 1934, it was inevitable that the design of the Rugby plant would be heavily influenced by the French equivalent. The entire construction was therefore in the hands of the Worcester firm, as sole contractors. This firm (being experts in the field) also supplied all five hydraulic dynamometers (brakes), each capable of absorbing 1200hp and operating at engine speeds between 15mph and 130mph. The test plant itself consisted of seven pairs of rollers supporting the locomotive, up to five of which were driven by the coupled wheels of the engine. The plant therefore had a theoretical capacity of 6000hp, though it was rated on opening at 4500hp.

The site selected for the station was adjacent to the motive power depot and locomotive repair shops of the LMS at Rugby. Other locations had been considered but this one was reasonably accessible from London and the Derby, Crewe and Doncaster workshops of the LMS and LNER, while the former Great Central line of the LNER passed close to the chosen plot, and a direct connection to this was envisaged.

At the outbreak of war in 1939 work was well advanced on the construction of the buildings, but in early 1940 progress was suspended. In 1944 the project was resumed, and DW Sandford was appointed Superintending Engineer until he relinquished his post due to ill health in early 1948, and was succeeded by DR Carling. The main building was 171ft long and 130ft wide and stood in 8 acres of ground, leaving ample room for expansion if required. Originally costed at £150,000, it had risen to £220,000 on completion, mostly as a result of the increased cost of materials and equipment following the war; it was finally opened on 19th October 1948.

Strangely, one engine arrived at the Rugby Testing Station before it was opened, was stored in the preparation shed adjacent to the plant itself for almost three years, was not used at all, and was only steamed for boiler examinations! The engine in question was a former North Eastern Railway S class 4-6-0, built in 1906 and taken out of traffic by the LNER in 1930 as class B13 1699. It was then rebuilt as a counter-pressure locomotive for testing purposes and used, in conjunction with the LNER dynamometer car, during the 1930s and 1940s. It was taken from Darlington to Rugby by Carling in anticipation of it taking part in the acceptance trials of the new station. Arriving at Rugby shed in July 1948, it was soon transferred to the new building. In the event, it left Rugby, unused, on 17th May 1951 for breaking up at Crewe.

The opening of the testing station therefore took place after Nationalisation, and long after Sir Nigel Gresley's death in 1941. His LMS co-founder Sir William Stanier was present, however, as were a galaxy of the "great and the good" in locomotive circles. All were arrayed in the yard in front of A4 60007 *Sir Nigel Gresley* and "Coronation" 46256 *Sir William A. Stanier, F.R.S.* to mark the fulfilment of the project first mooted 21 years earlier.

The A4 had arrived at Rugby prior to the opening, and was given trial runs on the rollers for three days as a prelude to the opening on the 19th October. On this day the Rt Hon Alfred Barnes, Minister of Transport, performed the official ceremony in the company of members of the British Transport Commission, the Railway Executive, the Trades Union Congress, representatives from overseas railways, the local MP and 50 members of the press. 60007 was run up to 62mph on the plant after the ceremony for demonstration purposes, and was both filmed and televised!

After this, the staff began the lengthy process of running-in the equipment and familiarising themselves with procedures. Understandably, this took some considerable time. The Superintending Engineer, DR Carling had come from Darlington, and had been heavily involved in road tests with the NER counter-pressure 4-6-0 and the NER dynamometer car. His assistant was HC Ockwell, whose background was in the testing team at Swindon and their GWR dynamometer car. In this respect Swindon had an advantage over Rugby in that the staff who tested the locomotives on the test plant at Swindon also conducted the follow-up road tests. At Swindon, SO Ell was in charge and ran an integrated and coherent test programme (built up over the years) that Rugby couldn't match for some time. It had been originally intended that one of the occupants of the preparation shed would be Rugby's own dynamometer car, and that Rugby would operate in the same manner as Swindon. However this was not to be, and post-Rugby road tests were carried out by staff at Derby, where the LMS No 1 dynamometer car was housed, and shortly the No 3 car as well (plus the Mobile Test Units – see page 39). This arrangement required an extra layer of liaison, and inevitably some difficulties arose as a result.

The total staff at the Locomotive Testing Station numbered 30 in all, though throughout the 12 years 1948-1959 inclusive there were only three weeks in which a full complement was actually achieved! When an engine was being tested, three people were generally in the cab, a driver, fireman and a "footplate observer" from the testing staff. The driver and fireman were often on long-term secondment (6 months) from the adjacent motive power depot, and once he'd got the engine running at the speed required for the test the

driver had very little to do. Not so the fireman however whose work was constant and hard, often so hard that a second, supplementary fireman was also employed to shovel coal fast enough! The tests themselves were of differing duration, varying from 70-80 minutes for a high-power test, to two hours plus for a test at low steaming rates. During these periods steady conditions simply had to be maintained, rigorously, for the test to be valid and the partnership between fireman and footplate observer was therefore the linchpin of locomotive testing at Rugby.

There would generally be two testing sessions per day, one in the morning and one in the afternoon. Then, the engine would be allowed to gradually "run-down" to use up most of the existing fire and make disposal easier. After this, it would be disconnected from the cab drawbar dynamometer, and all the associated testing pipework removed. The running

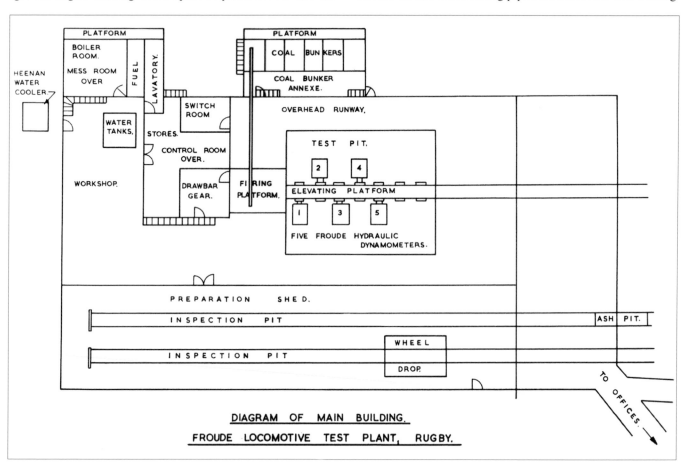

Above: Plan of the Rugby Testing Station. (National Railway Museum/SSPL)

Opposite page, top: An elevated view of the incomplete Rugby Testing Station. The office block (left) is still being built, and trackwork into the preparation shed next door has yet to be finished. The viaduct carried the GC main line, with Leicester to the left and Marylebone to the right. The line receding into the distance is that to Peterborough (via Stamford). 23rd September 1948. (National Railway Museum/SSPL)

Opposite page, bottom: The main control room was behind the large glass window seen in the photograph on page 28, and was heavily sound-proofed. The dials seen here controlled the Froude brakes, and the upright "clock" displayed the (equivalent) engine speed. One of the LMS "Black Fives" 44765 is running on the plant down below. 29th August 1950. (National Railway Museum/SSPL)

rail was then raised and the rollers lowered so that the engine could move off the plant under its own steam for the fire to be dropped outside and the ash removed from the smokebox before retiring for the night into the preparation shed. This is where the engine's tender was stored while testing took place, as all coal and water supplied during the tests was carefully and accurately recorded, the coal being fed into the firebox from a firing platform, adjustable in height to suit each locomotive. (The coal itself was brought directly from the colliery to the testing station by special delivery. Specific types of coal would be ordered and the resident chemist had the task of analysing its composition – ash content for instance – and measuring its calorific value, before any test.) The following morning the procedures would be reversed. If things were going well, near the end of any complete test, the next locomotive on the schedule would arrive at the preparation shed a few days in advance to ensure that necessary checks as to the condition of the engine could be made. The outgoing engine would usually be reunited with its tender and be sent back into service within a few days.

At the end of 1959, testing of steam engines ceased and the Rugby plant was effectively mothballed. Carling was seconded to the Research & Experiments office of the International Union of Railways (IUR), and other staff were dispersed to various Regional posts. Ockwell, however, remained on site with a small nucleus of maintenance staff. A handful of diverse tests took place thereafter until 1965, one of which (involving gas turbine 18000) being at the instigation of Carling through his work for the IUR! The equipment itself was dismantled in 1970 and the buildings demolished in 1984.

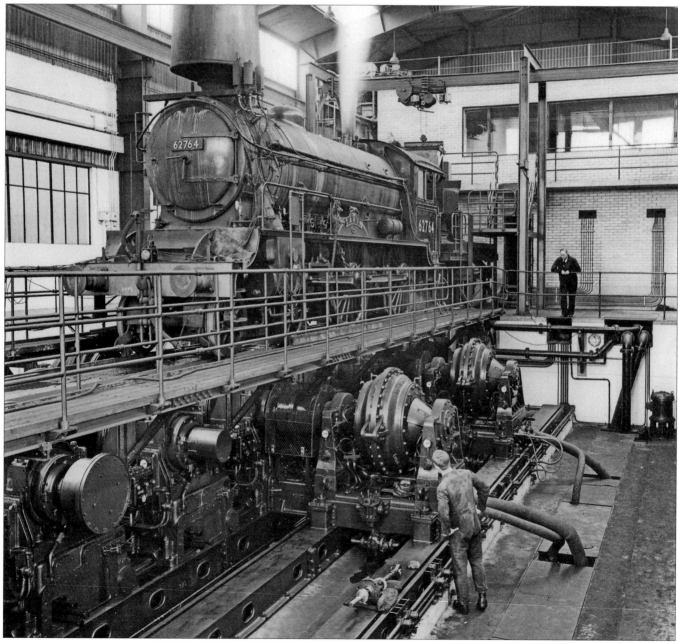

1948	16th to 18th October	A4 4-6-2 60007 *Sir Nigel Gresley*, makes trial runs prior to opening
	19th October	A4 4-6-2 60007 *Sir Nigel Gresley*, non-test runs to 62mph on opening day, runs 150 miles in total over the 4 days
	26th November to 3rd December	WD 2-10-0 73799, makes 5 trial runs
	8th to 22nd December	WD 2-10-0 73799, performs acceptance trials
1949	5th to 14th January	WD 2-10-0 73799, further acceptance trials and calibration of Amsler equipment
	24th January to 9th February	Class 5 4-6-0 44752, acceptance tests for CME, LMR, running up to 90mph
	21st February to 13th April	WD 2-10-0 73799, equipment tests
	26th April to 6th May	WD 2-10-0 73788, further equipment tests
	7th May to 1st June	D49 4-4-0 62764 *The Garth*, investigation of infinitely variable poppet valves, locomotive suffers failure. On 10th May there was a visit from the Institution of Locomotive Engineers. On 31st May there was a Press visit.
	8th to 10th June	WD 2-10-0 73788, further equipment tests
	14th to 29th June	D49 4-4-0 62764 *The Garth*, more poppet valve tests after repairs
	26th to 28th July	WD 2-10-0 73788, further equipment tests
	3rd to 11th August	D49 4-4-0 62764 *The Garth*, final tests up to 80mph
	21st October to 19th December	WD 2-10-0 73788, final equipment tests
1950	3rd January to 19th May	Class 5 4-6-0 45218, investigation of valve event settings. On 18th May, there was a live BBC radio broadcast at high speed.
	2nd June to 4th October	Class 5 4-6-0 44765, performance with various dimensions of single/double chimneys up to 75mph (see photograph on page 27)
	12th to 31st October	Class 5 4-6-0 44862, efficiency tests with dirty boiler. On 24th October there was a visit of ASLEF/NUR representatives.
	13th to 23rd November	B1 4-6-0 61353, engine tests with clean boiler
	29th November to 8th January 1951	Class 5 4-6-0 44862, engine tests, clean boiler
1951	15th January to 30th March	B1 4-6-0 61353, performance and efficiency tests. On 16th March there was a visit by members of the Railway Executive and the "Coal Working Party".
	17th April to 28th May	7MT 4-6-2 70005 *John Milton*, performance and efficiency tests with live exhaust steam injectors. On 18th May there was a visit by the Technical Press.
	7th June to 1st August (Closed for annual holidays from 28th June to 17th July)	B1 4-6-0 61353, performance and efficiency tests, then controlled road tests, Carlisle to Skipton for Bulletin 2. On 21st June there was a visit by the Cambridge University Railway Club.
	13th August to 5th November	5MT 4-6-0 73008, performance and efficiency tests with live exhaust steam injectors. "Farnboro" indicator first used on 25th October.
	3rd December to 22nd January 1952	7MT 4-6-2 70005 *John Milton*, performance and efficiency tests, then controlled road tests, Carlisle to Skipton for Bulletin 5. On 20th December and 8th January, both days were given over to filming and no tests took place.

Opposite page: *After various equipment tests had been completed, the first engine to undergo actual testing was one of Gresley's D49 class, designed for secondary passenger service and the only 4-4-0 ever tested. It was fitted with poppet valves (rather than piston valves) and was at Rugby to evaluate the performance of these. 62764 "The Garth" was named after one of the famous Hunts of the day and a casting of a fox can be seen above the nameplate. As the locomotive is blowing off, testing must be finished for the day, since it was almost a criminal offence to allow the safety valves to lift whilst on test. The photograph was taken between May and August 1949. (National Railway Museum/SSPL)*

1952	30th January to 21st February	5MT 4-6-0 73008, performance and efficiency tests (a record 271 "miles" were run in a day on the rollers), then controlled road tests, Carlisle to Skipton for Bulletin 6
	19th March to 2nd October	8P 4-6-2 35022 *Holland America Line*, performance and efficiency tests up to 90mph, then controlled road tests, Carlisle to Skipton for Bulletin 10. A steam rate of 42,000lb/hr was achieved. On 12th/13th August, both days were given over to filming and no tests took place.
	31st October to 20th February 1953	7MT 4-6-2 70025 *Western Star*, performance test and indicator comparison. On 16th December there was a visit by the President of the Institution of Mechanical Engineers.
1953	10th March to 7th May	8P 4-6-2 35022 *Holland America Line*, performance with single blastpipe and chimney (photograph, page 32). Chimney heights also altered.
	22nd July to 3rd November	5MT 4-6-0 73030, engine tests, with various blastpipe diameters and various grades of coal
	25th to 27th November	7MT 4-6-2 70025 *Western Star*, demonstration runs for TV programme with Richard Dimbleby
	15th December to 26th January 1954	8P 4-6-2 35022 *Holland America Line*, boiler tests without thermic syphons in firebox using the boiler from 35014
1954	10th February to 30th April	5MT 2-6-0 42725, performance tests with piston valves
	7th May to 20th August	9F 2-10-0 92013, performance and efficiency tests (photograph, page 33), then controlled road tests, Carlisle-Skipton for Bulletin 13. 25th June – filming day.
	31st August to 1st October	5MT 2-6-0 42725, further tests with piston valves
	12th to 27th October	9F 2-10-0 92015, tests with modified regulator
	8th November to 7th January 1955	5MT 2-6-0 42824, performance tests fitted with Reidinger poppet valves. On one run the engine was out of control with its speed rising!
1955	31st January to 16th May	8P 4-6-2 46225 *Duchess of Gloucester*, performance and efficiency tests, then controlled road tests, Carlisle to Skipton (though not until March-May 1956). Numerous tests were curtailed due to slipping – in one case to 110mph. A steam rate of 41,700lb/hr was achieved.
	7th June to 28th September	9F 2-10-0 92023, performance and efficiency tests fitted with Crosti boiler (photograph, page 34), then controlled road tests, Carlisle-Hurlford. Dr Crosti visited on 20th July and 18th, 22nd, 23rd August. RC Bond visited on 4th August. ES Cox visited on 22nd August.
	7th October to 15th November	9F 2-10-0 92050, performance and efficiency tests and indicator comparisons, then controlled road tests, Carlisle to Hurlford (Bulletin 13 covers 92013/50)
	7th December to 25th May 1956	7P 4-6-0 46165 *The Ranger 12th London Regt*, performance tests up to 90mph and improvement to steaming. Many tests abandoned due to slipping or loss of water.
1956	15th June to 28th September	5MT 2-6-0 42824, performance tests with modified Reidinger poppet valves
	5th October to 26th February 1957	6P 4-6-0 45722 *Defence*, double blastpipe and chimney tests to improve steaming with poorer coals. Many tests abandoned due to slipping or loss of water.
1957	6th March to 26th April	9F 2-10-0 92050, further engine tests for controlled road test indicator reconciliation. The Regional Board visited on 7th March.
	22nd July to 13th January 1958	4-6-0 GT3, a private-venture gas turbine by English Electric – development work (photograph, page 35). A demonstration run for the Chief Engineer of English Electric was held on 16th August. RC Bond visited, 12th September. ES Cox visited, 21st October. HG Nelson Esq visited, 12th November.

1958	11th February to 31st October	5MT 4-6-0 73031, tests with increased superheat
	21st November to 19th March 1959	9F 2-10-0 92166, performance tests while fitted with Berkley mechanical stoker
1959	9th April to 1st September	9F 2-10-0 92250, evaluation tests with double chimney and Giesl ejector. Also tests with lower grade coal.

The official record held at the NRM ends here, with 92250 being the last steam engine to be tested on the plant. Thereafter, the station was manned by a skeleton staff and put on a "care and maintenance" basis through to January 1962.

Further explanatory notes and background information

1948/9 – Use of 2-10-0s 73799/88 (later renumbered 90774/64)

As the testing station had five pairs of rollers which could be driven by locomotives, it would obviously be advantageous if all of them could be run-in at the same time. However, in 1948 there were very few ten-coupled engines available. Apart from the unique 0-10-0 Lickey banker, only War Department 2-10-0s existed, and only a handful of these were yet in serviceable condition. 73799 was working from Kingmoor depot (Carlisle) and was transferred on loan to the CME at Rugby, arriving there on 10th July. It was returned north in August, only to retrace its steps in early October to commence duties in late November, giving way to 73788 in April 1949. This engine had been put through Eastleigh Works in late 1948, and was operating from Motherwell (after a spell at Grangemouth) when called to Rugby.

1950/1 – Cancellation of tests with different chimneys on B1 61353

It had initially been intended that this engine, built new at Darlington in September 1949, would be tested not only with its standard single chimney and blastpipe, but with three other systems besides. These were a Kylchap double chimney, a Lemaître multiple-jet exhaust, and an LMS-type double chimney. To this end, the smokebox was modified (in September 1950 at Darlington) to readily accommodate the other systems, 61353 arriving at Rugby retaining its as-built single chimney. In the event, pressure of work at Rugby caused the tests with alternative exhaust arrangements not to take place, and a short visit to Darlington in December restored the smokebox to the standard design for the class.

18th May 1951 – Visit of the Technical Press

To facilitate this visit, a special train was put on from Euston to Rugby and back. This was headed by "Britannia" 70009 *Alfred the Great*, and included the LMR No 1 dynamometer car (next to the engine) and ample catering provision. Prior to the return trip, 70009 and No 1 were taken to Northampton to turn on the triangle, which involved a hair-raising 60mph dash, backwards, propelling the dynamometer car! Periods of 90mph running were a feature of the southbound run.

25th October 1951 – First use of the "Farnboro" indicator on 73008

An indicator is a piece of equipment for measuring the differing steam pressure in the cylinder throughout the length of the piston stroke. These values are usually recorded as a series of dots on a diagram, through which a curve can be drawn and from the area within this closed curve, the power produced by the engine (the "indicated horsepower") can be calculated. Until the coming of automatic, electrically-activated indicators when out on road tests, personnel had to sit or lie on the engine's running plate and hand-feed pieces of card into the recording device. This had to be close to the indicator, which was itself fixed to the cylinder ends. To protect the staff, temporary wooden shelters ("indicator shelters") were provided across the front, and for some distance along the sides, of the engine under test. These shelters appear in a number of the photos.

However, Rugby Testing Station gradually developed an electrical system based on the one that had originated at the Royal Aircraft Establishment at Farnborough for testing piston-driven aero-engines. This development became known as the "Farnboro" indicator, and it did not require the use of shelters when a locomotive was being subjected to a controlled road test. Some of the later tests with 70025 on the plant (1952/3) were used to compare the results from the Farnboro indicator with those obtained from the type used at Swindon, for which purpose a group of Swindon personnel visited Rugby bringing with them their own mechanical version. Both types were then used on the same engine at the same time.

1953/4 – Tests without thermic syphons in the firebox of 35022

A pair of Nicholson thermic syphons (supplied by Beyer Peacock) was provided in "Merchant Navy" class fireboxes. Their purpose was to promote efficient water circulation within the boiler, and enhance steam production. They were in effect large water tubes extending into the firebox itself, where conditions were hottest and where water could be turned into steam the quickest. They also helped to support the brick arch within the firebox. Comparative tests with, and without these syphons cast doubt on their effectiveness, but when the engines were rebuilt (from 1956) it was not considered economically viable to go to the expense of both removing them and fitting new brick arches. The use of these syphons on BR was confined to this class, the smaller "West Country" and "Battle of Britain" SR Pacifics and the short-lived "Leader" 36001.

June-September 1955 – Tests with a Crosti boiler on 92023

This device found widespread application on Italian Railways, and was designed (by Dr Crosti) to be fitted in one of two ways. In Italy, most frequently, two pre-heater drums (effectively extra boilers) were used, one on each side of the main boiler, both of which used the spent hot gases from the main boiler to preheat the water from the tender before it entered the main boiler. Alternatively, only one drum would be used, fitted below the main boiler, but which served the same purpose.

92023 was one of only ten locomotives (92020-29) built at Crewe in 1955 that were fitted experimentally with this type of boiler. In its BR application, it consisted of a single feedwater pre-heater slung beneath a conventional boiler. The hot gases from the top (conventional) boiler exited into

the smokebox as usual, but did not go out through the front chimney (which was closed except when lighting-up) but turned back on themselves and passed through the second, lower, boiler (the pre-heater drum) before finally exhausting through a chimney located alongside the top boiler, on the right-hand side just in front of the firebox. The pre-heated water thus entered the top boiler (at the front) much hotter than was customary, which allowed the conventional boiler to be of smaller dimensions, though pitched higher than usual. The final chimney was of a narrow, oblong design so as to impede the fireman's forward view as little as possible.

The engine's unconventional appearance was further added to by having two smokebox doors, one above the other, when viewed from the front. For various reasons, the hoped-for economy in coal consumption did not materialise, and the ten engines had the pre-heaters removed between December 1959 and June 1962. However, after 92023 had been tested,

The footplate scene during one of many tests with 35022 "Holland America Line". The driver (left) has very little to do (or see!), the fireman is busy as usual and the "footplate observer" (RTS staff) is John Click, who worked the injectors and kept an eye on all gauges to ensure stable conditions for the test. March 1953. (National Railway Museum/SSPL)

Dr Crosti's financial backers contested the results. (It had been hoped to sell many of such boilers to BR with a sliding scale of remuneration to Dr Crosti's backers depending on the percentage economy achieved.) DR Carling appointed the famous French engineer André Chapelon as arbiter. Having studied the test results carefully, he concluded on 26th November 1957 in favour of Rugby, and congratulated Carling on the accuracy and thoroughness of the testing procedures.

January-May 1955 and March-May 1956 – Tests with 46225

This engine arrived at Rugby immediately following a general repair, and then ran 7,205 miles on the plant under test conditions. During these tests there was some trouble with slipping at high power outputs, with the cylinder relief valves blowing and with the safety valves lifting below correct pressure. Despite this, 100 mph was reached on the rollers without slipping.

The loco was then released to the LMR Operating Department for summer timetable work. It was not called back for controlled road tests until the following Spring, after a heavy intermediate repair, and a further 4,600 miles were covered, culminating in the haulage of a 640-ton test train over the Settle & Carlisle line. Speed restrictions on this line limited the maximum speed to 80mph.

Unfortunately, the road test results showed a power output disagreement with those obtained at Rugby, and this took some considerable time to resolve. It was therefore not until July 1958 before report 13 was compiled as a final analysis, though the expected bulletin was never issued.

Dec 1955 to May 1956 and Oct 1956 to Feb 1957 – Tests with 46165 and 45722

Both these locos were subjected to tests at Rugby following complaints from the LMR Motive Power Department about poor steaming. In the case of 46165, this had been fitted with self-cleaning plates in the smokebox, and improved draughting arrangements were necessary to rectify their

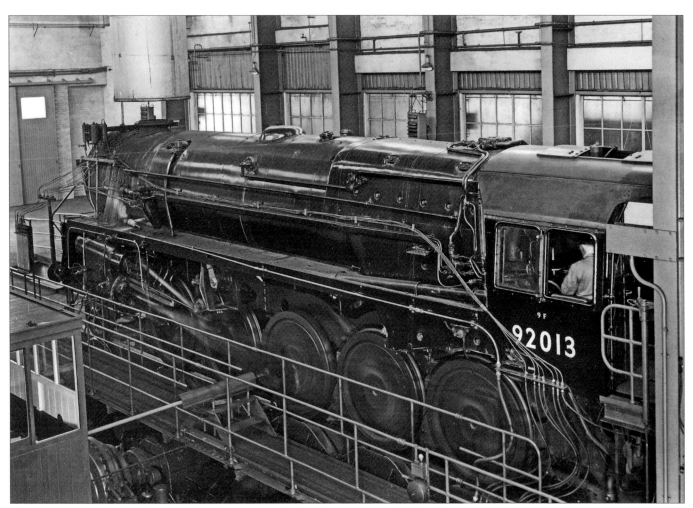

In 1954, 92013, almost new and with the smoke deflector plates removed, was the first of no less than six 9F 2-10-0s to grace the rollers for various reasons. The cabin on the left contained the "Farnboro" indicator, with the drive shaft connecting this to the engine's centre driving wheel clearly visible. June 1954. (National Railway Museum/SSPL)

detrimental effect on steaming. These modifications were subsequently fitted to at least 14 "Scots", but whether self-cleaning plates were also fitted is not known. The internal report on the tests states that, "As evidenced by the boiler characteristics, this class of engine is frequently overworked in daily service and complaints from the Motive Power Department giving rise to this testing and improvement are almost entirely traceable to this"!

The "Jubilee" class was not fitted with self-cleaning plates, and here the complaint arose from top-class coal not being available. Although the Locomotive Testing Committee minuted the request on 11th February 1955, tests were not undertaken until October 1956. When these were completed the remodelled draughting (with either single or double chimneys) increased the potential power output of the engine by 1/3, even with the lower grade fuel, and with better combustion. However, only relatively few of this large class

(numbering 192) are believed to have subsequently received the modified single chimney. Internal report R11 presented the relevant details.

1957/8 – Development tests with GT3

This locomotive ran 5,070 miles on the test plant, including one run at up to 90mph, though lubrication problems were frequently encountered. There was a demonstration run on 16th August 1957 for the English Electric Co's Chief Engineer, and visits were also made by RC Bond and ES Cox. After testing, GT3 remained on site for a further six months.

There were already two gas turbines locomotives running on the WR, 18000 and 18100. These had been built by Brown-Boveri in Switzerland and Metropolitan Vickers in Manchester respectively, and had been in service from 1950 (18000) and 1952 (18100). The former was rated at 2500hp

92023 was a 9F fitted with a Crosti boiler, on which the engine's chimney was well back towards the cab on the right-hand side. The test plant chimney therefore had to be moved to match this, and was considerably enlarged at the base to capture the offset exhaust from the unconventional chimney position. The "coal truck in the air" visible above the cab delivered weighed amounts of coal to the firing platform from the bunker outside the main building. July 1955.
(National Railway Museum/SSPL)

with an A1A-A1A wheel arrangement, and the latter was a 3000hp Co-Co. Both had electric transmissions, and could be regarded as GT1 and GT2, though this nomenclature was never applied to them. Nor at this stage in its development was "GT3" applied to the experimental engine that went to Rugby in July 1957, though it was also aimed at the WR. It was a private venture by English Electric at Vulcan Foundry, had mechanical transmission, was rated at 2750hp and (most surprisingly) was mounted on a BR 5MT chassis with a 4-6-0 wheel arrangement, plus a six-wheeled tender. The power unit was at a development stage and was brought to Rugby to try and iron out quite a number of teething problems.

It was returned to EE for further work, and eventually ran trials on BR in 1961 (now labelled GT3) though on the LMR, not on the WR. Although these trials were basically successful, the venture came too late for BR to take an interest, and the locomotive was scrapped in 1966.

February to October 1958 – Tests with 73031

These tests were the only ones conducted at the behest of the Research Department, Engineering Division (Derby). Their purpose was to investigate the relationship between increased superheat and cylinder efficiency. To this end, supplementary electric heating was provided to the superheater elements to show the effects of higher steam temperatures to the cylinders at low rates of working. The current for these elements was supplied by a 350hp diesel electric shunting engine positioned in the preparation shed adjacent to the test plant, with supply cables running between this loco and 73031! These heating effects should not only increase cylinder efficiency, but also reduce coal consumption.

The report concluded that further tests be conducted with longer elements and a Giesl-type chimney together with some form of "damping" device to block off a variable proportion

The first non-steam motive power unit to use the Rugby facility was the private venture gas turbine promoted by English Electric. This was still in the development stage, and differed considerably from the two WR gas turbines. When its brown-liveried bodywork was fitted it presented quite an attractive appearance. 1957.
(National Railway Museum/SSPL)

of the boiler tubes automatically as service demands dictated, but these tests were not carried out.

1958/9 – Tests with 92166

A Berkley mechanical stoker was fitted to three engines of this class (92165/6/7), although it had originally been intended to equip five. Designed to increase steam production beyond the capacity of one fireman, there were actually very few occasions when this was necessary (even on Birmingham-Carlisle fitted freights). The result was that coal consumption was higher than on hand-fired engines, and although fitted to these new engines in 1958, the stokers were removed in 1962. The only other application in BR practice had been to fit "Merchant Navy" 35005 *Canadian Pacific* with similar equipment between 1948 and 1951.

April to September 1959 – Double chimney and ejector tests with 92250

The Giesl ejector is a special type of chimney, highly efficient in producing smokebox vacuum and reducing back-pressure in the cylinders. It can also reduce coal consumption and increase the power of the locomotive. It was invented by the Austrian engineer Dr Giesl-Gieslingen and first fitted to an Austrian locomotive in 1951. The "chimney" has seven blastpipe nozzles in-line at the base and is therefore narrow in profile, tapering outwards from the base. Popular in some European countries and others world-wide, it was first offered to BR in 1954, but rejected.

Only after five years of persuasion (and mounting positive evidence from other railways) did BR relent and allow an example to be tested at Rugby. Although the ejector lived up to its promise under test, BR had effectively set its face against further development of the steam engine and cancelled the tests on the three other ejectors offered for trials on other classes, to the disappointment of Dr Giesl. One device had been sold to the narrow-gauge Talyllyn Railway in 1958, and in May 1962, BR(SR) fitted another to the unrebuilt Pacific 34064 *Fighter Command*, with impressive results, although the Region's requests for more were turned down by BR. 9F 92250 retained its ejector until withdrawal, and the NCB went on to purchase about 50 examples over the next few years. Much later, the preserved Keighley & Worth Valley Railway fitted two more, one to 34092 *City of Wells* and another to 2-6-0 78022, both in the 1980s.

Post-1959 use of the Locomotive Testing Station

Observations regarding the use of the plant, and the site, in the years after 1959 are few and far between, but the following are available.

1960	24th April	Inside preparation shed: D2909, 49293, 49342. Outside the plant: 10201, 61809.
1961	22nd May	Gas Turbine 18000 was noted in the preparation shed, having arrived from Market Harborough. This locomotive was the 1949 2500hp A1A-A1A gas turbine built by Brown-Boveri in Switzerland for WR service from 1950, and officially withdrawn by BR in December 1960, but put in store at Market Harborough. After Rugby it transferred back to Switzerland (via the Harwich-Zeebrugge train ferry) for further use (after rebuilding) for continued wheel/rail adhesion tests, only one axle being powered. These tests lasted until 1975, when 18000 (it was never re-numbered) travelled to Vienna, where all the instrumentation was removed. It then languished outside the Mechanical Engineering Testing building, but was finally brought back to Britain and currently resides at the Crewe Heritage Centre.
1962	24th March	18000 was still in the preparation shed, together with 46201 *Princess Elizabeth*, this being the subject of a preservation appeal
	Unknown date	E2001 used the plant for adhesion tests, using one axle only. This loco was formerly the Metropolitan Vickers 1951-built, 3000hp gas turbine Co-Co 18100, used on the WR, converted into an AC electric unit in 1958 for crew training on the Manchester-Crewe electrification scheme, and originally renumbered E1000. It was finally withdrawn in 1968 and scrapped in 1972. It had been several years since this loco and 18000 had been together in the same place!
1963	11th May	42854 and 44833 were seen outside the plant, with E2001 still in the preparation shed
	Unknown date	18000 used the plant for adhesion tests, initiated, it is believed, by DR Carling
1964		Nothing recorded

1965	23rd April	DMU power car used the plant for engine cooling system tests
	August	E2001 was employed on freight trains south of Crewe on several occasions
	1st Oct	The preparation shed contained class 5 locomotives 44860 and 44876 under repair. London Transport electric locomotives 2, 7, 16 and 18 were stored outside.
	Late 1965	Brush Bo-Bo *Hawk* underwent tests on the plant. This was originally the LMS-ordered, BR-built, 827hp diesel-electric 10800, completed by North British in 1950 and withdrawn in 1959. It became a research loco for a joint venture between BR and Brush into the use of alternating current in traction motors, and was re-equipped with a 1200hp Bristol/Maybach power unit. It operated tests on the GC main line between Leicester and Nottingham before and after its visit to Rugby, but finance ran out in 1968, and the engine was broken up in 1972. However, useful experience had been gained.
1966	Unknown date	*Hawk* left Rugby for tests between East Leake and Loughborough (Central) between 3rd and 25th January
	12th July	The London Transport locomotives noted above were cut up on site
1967	3rd June	E2001 was still present, together with ex-Morecambe & Heysham EMUs, M29027M and M28262M just outside the plant
1968	April	The preparation shed was used for fitting new bogies to loco-hauled coaching stock
1969		Nothing recorded
1970		The plant's equipment was dismantled. E2001 went to Akeman Street (near Princes Risborough). The buildings became a wagon repair shop for an unknown period of time before lying disused for some time. The offices, however, remained in use for planning the Weaver Junction to Glasgow electrification scheme.
1971 to 1975		Nothing recorded
1976		Records were removed from the offices and taken to new National Railway Museum at York
1977		Nothing recorded
1978	22nd February	A 3-car PEP EMU was noted outside the main building
1979 to 1983		Nothing recorded
1984		Work began to demolish the buildings at the end of September, and all had gone completely within a month. The area was then given over to industrial redevelopment.

The LMS corridor tender (described in Chapter 7) did not serve the same function as the better-known examples associated with the LNER A4 Pacifics. Here, the corridor enabled the testing staff to move between the dynamometer car and the footplate, although the narrow passage exited into the loose coal space rather than to the footplate itself, and was on the left-hand side (facing forwards), unlike the A4 tenders. 23rd October 1947. (National Railway Museum/SSPL)

Chapter 7

The Mobile Test Plant of the LMS

First proposed in 1936, and approved in 1937, this was a five-vehicle formation that comprised a special tender to attach to the locomotive being tested, a new dynamometer car and three mobile braking units. Although construction began in 1937, the intervention of the Second World War caused considerable delay, and the full set was not finally complete until after nationalisation.

Brake unit 2 was finished first, and ran trials in 1938/9, but the special tender and brake units 1 and 3 were not ready until 1947. The dynamometer car not finished 1949, and therefore saw no LMS use at all. When built, the purpose of this multi-part train was to conduct constant-speed road tests of the steam locomotives of the LMS, though provision was made within the car for instrumentation to be provided later for the testing of diesel or electric engines as well.

It is worthwhile, at this point, to give some description of each of these specialised vehicles.

The corridor tender, completed 1947

This was ordered from Crewe Works in 1937, and a standard "Black Five" tender chassis (numbered 9073, and allocated to new class 5 No 5012) was taken out of sequence, renumbered 4999 and converted to a 3,500 gallon tender with special features. These included a coal space divided longitudinally, the left-hand one holding 3 tons of loose coal and the right-hand one being a space for 3 tons of pre-weighed coal in hundredweight bags. It was this coal that was brought forward and only used during testing. A small steam-powered winch was also provided to hoist the bags into the tender. Additionally, the water supplied to the boiler was metered (and could be read in the dynamometer car) and it had a corridor running through it on the left-hand side (facing forwards) so that personnel could transfer from the footplate to the dynamometer car and vice versa, by means of the gangway connections at the ends of each vehicle. From this it can be seen that all coal and water consumed by the engine on test could be easily measured. The tender was initially painted red and lettered LMS, but at some time between the tests with 90772 (1952) and those with 44981 (1954) it was repainted into standard BR lined black livery.

In service, it was used infrequently, and only eight locomotives (six of them class 5s) were tested when coupled to this tender, which otherwise lay idle. Consequently, it was rebuilt with a standard 4,000 gallon tank in November 1959, the special features were removed and it was then paired with class 5 No 45235 until this engine was withdrawn in January 1966, when the tender was transferred to another class 5 No 44671 until this was itself scrapped, along with the tender.

The new No 3 Dynamometer Car, completed 1949

This was called No 3 due to its LMS lineage – No 1 being the

L&YR (Horwich) car on which the LMS was then relying, and No 2 being the LNWR (Crewe) car which had been converted into a flange-force testing car. No 3 retained this name under BR ownership, and its running number was M45049 on the London Midland Region. The main designs were prepared before his retirement by Sir William Stanier and finalised by HG Ivatt, his successor. It was built at Derby, the underframe in the Locomotive Works, the body and bogies in the Carriage & Wagon shops, and was 60ft long. The main recording table was supplied by Messrs Alfred Amsler & Sons of Schaffhausen, Switzerland, who also made the hydraulic dynamometer itself. These expensive items (£5,150 12s 0d at 1938 prices!) had been ordered pre-war, and part of the delay in finishing the car was due to the difficulty in transporting them in the immediate post-war period, together with a lack of sufficient foreign exchange for payment, this being in short supply at the time.

The car was built for the dual purpose of carrying out variable-speed testing on service trains (for which purpose it was used solo), or of working in conjunction with the mobile brake units for constant-speed testing. This latter style of testing was soon superseded by "constant rate of steaming" tests, but the instrumentation was equally suited to either method. Roller-bearing axleboxes were fitted, permitting speeds of up to 120mph, though at the time of its introduction very little mileage was authorised to be covered at more than 85mph. When used in conjunction with brake units, the car contained the master controls for the electronic regulation of the braking load in each unit. It was also fitted for indicating cylinders via electronic means, from the outset.

In the mid-1950s, the car was re-equipped with electrical instruments for the testing of diesel and electric locomotives, and later still it was adapted for multi-channel electrical recording. From 1969 (now known as Test Car No 3) it became the main vehicle for use in high-speed testing, and carried out the first tests in Great Britain at 125mph in 1970. In 1972, it received a dual-braking system (air and vacuum) for use with the prototype HST, recording the 143mph dash between York and Darlington in 1973, after which came graceful retirement into the National Collection. This vehicle therefore still exists, and after spending several years outstationed by the NRM at Barrow Hill, Chesterfield it was moved in June 2011 to the Midland Railway Centre at Butterley.

The Mobile Test Units (MTUs)

Before construction of these vehicles had even begun, preliminary experiments were put in hand to provide information about their basic design. To ascertain the probable riding characteristics when running at high speed, a train was made up to represent the test train as closely as possible. This consisted of engine 6205 *Princess Victoria*, No 2 dynamometer car, one standard coach, and a Manchester

-Bury electric motor coach. The latter was selected to mimic as nearly as possible the proportions (in terms of weight distribution) of the proposed braking units. Tests were made on 29th August 1937 between Crewe and Rugby at different speeds up to 90 mph.

The initial literature refers to these vehicles as "brake" units (as was their function) but once built they had the legend "Mobile Test Unit" painted on the side, and are henceforth referred to as MTUs Nos 1, 2 and 3.

The three vehicles were outwardly similar, and each had four 375hp air-cooled generators driven from the axles. Each unit could therefore absorb 1500hp on a continuous basis, though No 1 was geared for a maximum speed of 50mph, No 2 for 90mph and No 3 for 120mph. These MTUs could be used singly, in pairs, or all together according to the speed and brake force required for the individual tests. They were controlled automatically from the dynamometer car, and provided whatever braking power was necessary, either to keep the speed constant or to artificially increase the load behind the engine (rather than employ an increasingly long train!) If desired, each could also be controlled manually from within the unit itself.

Only MTU No 2 was completed pre-war, being turned out from Derby C&W shops at the end of November 1938. Research vehicle 198513 was temporarily fitted with the electronic master controls (supplied by British Thomson-Houston of Rugby) and testing of the new control system began in early December. On the 5th, a Derby-Burton-Leicester-Derby circuit was completed with manual control of No 2, while on the 9th (in great secrecy) electronic control was initiated – successfully. On the back of this, the Management Committee were, to their surprise, taken for a trip around the same circuit at different speeds with automatic control – an historic occasion. Further tests were made in 1939 with the No 2 LNWR car and MTU No 2 round the same circuit, and a total of 15 test runs were made in May/June, all behind 4F 0-6-0 4542.

The two remaining MTUs were completed in 1947, and pending the arrival in service of No 3 dynamometer car in 1949, the master controls for all three MTUs were placed in the No 1 dynamometer car. The first trial run of the complete Mobile Test Plant (less tender but with No 3 dynamometer car) was from Derby to Nottingham and back, and

took place on 22nd April 1949. The first actual locomotive test was with class 5 No 44764 (with corridor tender) between Derby and Willesden on 9th August 1949.

Whilst in service with the LMS and BR, the following details applied to the various testing vehicles:

Vehicle	Running Number	Weight	Maximum Speed	Notes
MTU No 1	M45053	66 tons	50 mph	gear ratio 16:91
MTU No 2	M45054	68t 17cwt	90 mph	gear ratio 27:86
MTU No3	M45055	69t 2cwt	120 mph	gear ratio 35:86
No 3 Dynamometer Car	M45049	42t 6cwt	120 mph	LMS/BR 1949
No 1 Dynamometer Car	M45050	32t 15cwt		L&YR 1913
No 2 Dynamometer Car	M45051			LNWR 1908

When not in use, all these vehicles were kept at Derby during the BR period.

The last full-scale performance test with No 3 dynamometer car and the MTUs concerned the Brush-built 4000hp diesel locomotive, *Kestrel*, and was conducted on 18th October 1968. From 1970 onwards, the three MTUs were used for diesel loco acceptance trials, but were retired from active service during 1974. MTU No1 was acquired by the NRM in 1978 and still exists, albeit in a parlous state.

Chapter 8

L&YR/LMS No 1 Dynamometer Car

This double-bogied vehicle replaced the Lancashire & Yorkshire Railway's earlier 4-wheeled car of 1896. The new car (L&YR 293) was to the design of George Hughes (CME 1904-1925) and was built in the Newton Heath Carriage Works, Manchester during 1911, before moving to Horwich Works for fitting out in 1912. It was ready for service in early 1913 equipped with a spring dynamometer, and was later overhauled and improved at Derby by the LMS in 1929, gaining a corridor connection at the train end, together with electric lighting and new instruments.

Pre-grouping use, significant runs only, 1913-1922

1913	7th February	L&YR 4-6-0 (4-cyl) 1506, Horwich-Hellifield via Bolton (out) and Chorley (return) – the car's first run
	26th February	L&YR 4-4-2 1392, demonstration run for John Aspinall (former CME), Liverpool-Manchester
	27th June	L&YR 4-6-0 1514, Sandhills-Colne with 12-coach LNWR Royal train
1918	21st July	L&YR 4-6-0 1506, Manchester-Blackpool, train timing
1919	19th to 21st July	On loan to Great Northern Railway for brake trials from Peterborough
1920	5th December	L&YR 4-6-0 1522, Horwich-Hellifield, 14 coaches plus the dynamometer car using a superheated engine
1921	21st August	LNWR 4-6-0 1351, Manchester-Blackpool, 14 coaches plus the dynamometer car using a superheated engine
	30th October	LNWR "Claughton" 4-6-0 192, Manchester-Blackpool, 17 coaches plus the dynamometer car For comparison with: L&YR 4-6-0 1521, Manchester-Blackpool, 17 coaches plus the dynamometer car
1922	1st January	L&YR and LNWR amalgamate
	13th, 14th June	L&YR Hughes 4-6-0 1657, Crewe-Carlisle, 13 coaches plus the dynamometer car using a superheated engine
1923	1st January	L&YR and LNWR become grouped into the LMS. The dynamometer car continues to be kept at Horwich Works

Post-grouping use, significant runs only, 1923-1939

1923	24th June	Double-headed 4-6-0s, Crewe-Carlisle and back hauling 500-ton train
	17th to 31st December	Compound 4-4-0 1008, 12.10pm Carlisle-Leeds via Settle & Carlisle route and 4.17pm return working. Results in LMS deciding to build more of these locomotives.
1924	23rd April	Compound 4-4-0 1011, 12.20pm Manchester-Derby service, both high and low pressure cylinders had indicator diagrams taken
	13th July	The Lickey incline banking engine, "Big Bertha", 0-10-0, tested on goods trains between Wellingborough and Brent
	16th to 19th December	"Big Bertha" 0-10-0, Compound 4-4-0 1065 and S&DJR 4-4-0 67 tested on goods trains between Bath and Bournemouth on S&DJR line

Opposite: Of the three MTUs, only No 2 was completed pre-war and ran tests in 1939. After one of these runs this interesting group shot was taken at Derby, with DW Sandford on the right (Superintending Engineer, RTS 1944-48) and HI Andrews (who developed the MTU principles) next to him; fourth from the right is RC Bond (then Superintending Engineer RTS, later British Railways Chief Officer – Locomotive Works) with ES Cox on his right (later BR Executive Officer – Design). (National Railway Museum/SSPL)

1925		Car now housed permanently at Derby, rather than Horwich. Renumbered 10874 in LMS lists.
1926	1st to 4th June	CR Pickersgill 4-6-0 14630, Carlisle-Preston and back
	16th to 19th November	GWR 4-6-0 5000 *Launceston Castle*, Crewe-Carlisle and back after appearing on revenue-earning trains between Crewe and Euston
1927	24th October to 8th December	4-6-0 6100 *Royal Scot*, Euston-Crewe, Euston-Carlisle and Glasgow (Central)-Carlisle return runs, "suspiciously" good results obtained! (Various dates, not continuous.)
1928	22nd March	On loan to LNER. A3 4-6-2s 2544 *Lemberg* (up) and 4473 *Solario* (down), Doncaster-Peterborough. Car coupled back-to-back with LNER car 902502 for comparison. Considerable discrepancies revealed. Car later repaired and modified at Derby.
	28th March to 12th April	"Ljungström" turbine loco – an experimental 2-6-0, Leeds-St Pancras
1929	1st to 5th, 26th and 28th November	4-4-0 587, Derby-Trent and Derby-Bristol return runs, first runs after overhaul
1930	27th to 30th May	S&DJR 2-8-0s 9674 and 9678, Wellow-Bath, on 530-ton freight
1932	29th May	2-6-6-2T Garratt 4967, Toton-Brent with a 1,340-ton train
	3rd July	2-6-6-2T Garratt 4999, Derby-Bedford, with coaching stock!
1932/3/4	Various dates	High pressure 4-6-0 6399 *Fury*, Derby-Trent and Derby-Wellingborough
1933		Car renumbered 45050
1934	5th to 13th September	New "Black Five" 4-6-0 5020, Crewe-Euston and return
	17th, 18th September	4-6-0 5553 *Canada*, Wolverhampton-Euston and return
	25th September to 1st October	4-6-0 5556 *Nova Scotia*, Wolverhampton-Euston and return
	11th, 12th December	Darlington-York, calibration tests with both LMS and LNER cars coupled together (locomotives unknown)
1935	19th to 23rd March	4-6-0 5051, Crewe-Euston, indicator tests
1936	Week beginning 4th May	4-6-2 6202 "Turbomotive" worked the "Royal Scot" between Euston and Glasgow with 470-560 ton loads
	16th, 17th November	4-6-2 6201 *Princess Elizabeth*, Euston-Glasgow high-speed non-stop tests with 225/255 tons. A world record time of 344 minutes for 401 miles was achieved.
	August/September	Car overhauled at Derby prior to CME inspection at Blackpool on 11th September
1937	12th to 15th October	4-6-0 5660 *Rooke*, Bristol-Leeds and Leeds-Glasgow (St Enoch), working to accelerated timings
	22nd to 25th November	4-6-2 6220 *Coronation* worked the "Coronation Scot" between Euston and Glasgow with 331 tons
1938	8th June	4-6-2 6225 *Duchess of Gloucester*, Euston-Glasgow in conjunction with the Institution of Locomotive Engineers' summer meeting in Glasgow, for the benefit of British and German members
1939	12th, 26th February	4-6-2 6234 *Duchess of Abercorn*, Crewe-Glasgow and return. On the up run on 26th February, a British record power output was recorded of 2511 dbhp (3348 ihp) with 604 tons behind

Post-war LMS use, 1944-1947

1944	12th to 15th December	4-6-0 6131 *The Royal Warwickshire Regiment*, Crewe-Carlisle
1945	6th to 9th March	4-6-0 6131 *The Royal Warwickshire Regiment*, Crewe-Carlisle, rebuilt with taper boiler
	1st to 4th May	4-6-0 5736 *Phoenix*, rebuilt "Jubilee" class, Crewe-Carlisle
	4th to 7th December	4-6-2 6252 *City of Leicester*, Crewe-Carlisle, coal and water tests
1946	12 days in March to July	2-6-4Ts 2648, 2207, 2230 and 2347, Southport-Manchester services (it was rare for tank engines to be tested)
1947	19th January	4-6-2 21C13 *Blue Funnel*, Brighton-Norwood, coal and water tests
	23rd January	4-6-2 21C139 *Boscastle*, Victoria-Dover (Marine), coal and water tests
	25th, 26th January	4-6-2 21C13 *Blue Funnel*, Waterloo-Exeter, coal and water tests
	30th March	4-6-2 21C156 *Croydon*, Brighton-Norwood Junction, coal and water tests
	15th to 18th April	2-6-0 6419, Crewe-Holyhead
	29th April to 8th May	On loan to LMS Research Department, Derby, for testing with new MTU No 1. Wind pressure and direction tests with Compound 4-4-0 1160 and 4-6-0s 4997, 4866 and 5419 between Rugby and Peterborough.

British Railways use, 1948-1967

1948	14th, 15th January	1600hp Co-Co 10000, 10.30am Derby-St Pancras and 12.15pm St Pancras-Manchester-Derby
	25th, 26th February	Calibration test with ex-GWR dynamometer car W7 at Derby prior to Interchange Trials (see Chapter 2)
	24th, 31st March	4-6-2 46246 *City of Manchester*, Rugby-Willesden with MTUs 2 and 3, wind pressure tests with anemometer
	20th April	4-6-2 46236 *City of Bradford*, Euston-Carlisle, Interchange Trials – first run
	10th September	WD 2-8-0 63149 (90490), Toton-Brent, Interchange Trials – last run
	Various days between 23rd September and 11th November	4-6-2 35005 *Canadian Pacific*, 10.50am Waterloo-Exeter "Atlantic Coast Express". Fitted with Berkley mechanical stoker – trials with different grades of coal. Total car mileage between 30th March 1947 and 11th November 1948: 22,428 miles.
1949	Various dates between 5th April and 25th May	2-6-0 43027, Crewe-Holyhead, trials with single and double blastpipe
	5th to 8th July	4-6-0 44757, St Pancras-Manchester, Caprotti valve gear and double chimney
	12th to 15th July	4-6-0 44764, St Pancras-Manchester, Walschaerts valve gear and single chimney
	19th to 21st July	4-6-0 44766, St Pancras-Manchester, Walschaerts valve gear and double chimney
	23rd to 26th August	4-6-0 44767, St Pancras-Manchester, Stephenson valve gear and double chimney
1950	13th to 23rd February	4-6-0 44816, 4-6-0 44819 and 4-6-0 44921, St Pancras-Nottingham and Somers Town-Ancoats, standardisation of freight train classification for all regions
	22nd, 30th June	827hp Bo-Bo 10800, Derby-Leicester-Manchester-Derby, acceptance trials
	7th, 12th, 26th September and 10th October	Unknown locomotive, Derby-Chinley-Derby, calibration runs with No 3 dynamometer car

1951	12th, 13th January	7MT 4-6-2 70000, 12.50pm Crewe-Carlisle and 11.52am return next day with a new and, as yet, unpainted and un-named engine
	23rd to 27th April	B1 4-6-0 61353, Carlisle-Skipton-Carlisle, controlled road tests after testing on Rugby test plant
	18th May	4-6-2 70009 *Alfred the Great*, Euston-Rugby-Euston, demonstration run for the technical press to visit Rugby test plant
	4th to 15th June	4-6-2 70005 *John Milton*, Carlisle-Skipton-Carlisle, controlled road tests after testing on Rugby test plant
	13th to 24th August	B1 4-6-0 61353, Carlisle-Skipton-Carlisle, controlled road tests after testing on Rugby test plant for Bulletin 2
	12th to 23rd November	5MT 4-6-0 73008, Carlisle-Skipton-Carlisle, controlled road tests after testing on Rugby test plant for Bulletin 2
	12th December	Unknown locomotive, Derby-Chinley-Derby, calibration runs with No 3 car
1952	28th January to 15th February	4-6-2 70005 *John Milton*, Carlisle-Skipton-Carlisle, controlled road tests after testing on Rugby test plant for Bulletin 5 (see frontispiece, page vi)
	3rd to 7th March	5MT 4-6-0 73008, Carlisle-Skipton-Carlisle, controlled road tests after testing on Rugby test plant for Bulletin 6
	27th October to 27th November	4-6-2 35022 *Holland America Line*, Carlisle-Skipton-Carlisle, controlled road tests after testing on Rugby test plant for Bulletin 10. Total car mileage between 5th April 1949 and 27th November 1952: 18,572 miles.
1953	Unknown date	Car repainted in carmine and cream livery
	29th September to 1st October	4-6-0 44738, Crewe-Shrewsbury, Caprotti valve gear, indicator tests
	29th October to 24th November	4-6-0 44678, repeat of 44738 tests, above
	15th December	0-6-0 44030, Crewe-Derby, calibration run with No 3 dynamometer car. Formation: 44030, No 1 car, No 3 car, MTU 1, MTU 2, van.
1954		Car not used
1955	12th May	2000hp 4-8-4 10100, "Fell" diesel mechanical, Carlisle-Skipton-Carlisle, paired with No 3 car
	15th to 23rd August	4-6-0 45636 *Uganda*, Nottingham-St Pancras, water treatment tests
	24th, 25th August	4-6-0 45610 *Gold Coast*, Nottingham-St Pancras, water treatment tests
	29th August to 8th September	4-6-0 45506 *The Royal Pioneer Corps*, Nottingham-St Pancras, water treatment tests
	12th to 21st September	4-6-0 44918, Nottingham-St Pancras, water treatment tests
1956/7/8		Car not used
1959	30th June, 1st July	1160hp Bo-Bo D5008, paired with No 3 car to measure output of train heating boiler on 15-coach train
	26th October to 6th November	0-6-0 44481, Walton-Rowsley, freight trials
1960	20th June	9F 2-10-0 92153 and 2300hp 1Co-Co1 D8 *Penyghent*, Toton-Brent, freight trials
	13th to 15th September	WD 2-8-0 90448, 90638 and 90237, Woodford Halse-Honeybourne, freight trials
	25th, 26th September	1160hp Bo-Bo D5091, Toton-Brent, freight trials
	2nd, 3rd October	4MT 4-6-0 75064, Toton-Brent, freight trials
	16th, 17th October	1200hp Co-Bo D5711, Toton-Brent, freight trials
	23rd, 30th October	1160hp Bo-Bo D5083, Buxton-Stockport, freight trials
	6th to 9th December	5MT 4-6-0 73144, Rowsley-Cheadle, freight trials

1961	7th, 8th February	2-8-0 48008, Rowsley-Cheadle, freight trials
	9th, 10th February	4-6-0 45260, Rowsley-Cheadle, freight trials
	14th, 15th February	2-6-0 42769, Rowsley-Cheadle, freight trials
	16th, 17th February	0-6-0 44262, Rowsley-Cheadle, freight trials
	24th April	1160hp Bo-Bo D5061, Rowsley-Gowhole, freight trials
	17th to 20th July	2500hp 1Co-Co1 D107 and brake tender, Beeston-Saxby, freight trials
	24th July to 3rd August	1160hp Bo-Bo D5089 and brake tender, Beeston-Saxby, Rowsley-Cheadle, freight trials
	14th August to 22nd September	2500hp 1Co-Co1 D45, D95 and D105, Rowsley-Cheadle, freight trials
1962	7th to 22nd March	1160hp Bo-Bo D5142, Derby-Chellaston, freight trials
	14th to 31st May	2500hp 1Co-Co1 D150 and brake tender, Derby-Rowsley-Cheadle and Beeston-Corby-Beeston, freight trials
	25th, 26th July	1160hp Bo-Bo D5084, Toton-Brent, freight trials
1963	18th, 19th August	2500hp 1Co-Co1 D119, Wigston-Brent-Derby, freight trials
1964	10th, 16th and 23rd January	1550hp Bo-Bo D6553, Derby-Knighton-Derby, test with Freightliner wagons
	2nd to 20th March	1160hp Bo-Bo D5142, Chellaston-Melbourne Junction-Derby, test with "hyfit" and "minfit" wagons
1965	22nd February to 11th April	2750hp Co-Co D1820, Chaddesden-Bedford, Derby-Spondon and Derby-Rowsley-Derby, Freightliner tests
	April to December	Car used as a brake van on Freightliner trains
1966	24th April	2500hp 1Co-Co1 D136, Toton-Kettering-Derby, freight trials
	1st, 5th May	2750hp Co-Co D1810, D1796, Ilkeston-Trowell with iron ore tipplers
	8th May	2750hp Co-Co D1835, Toton-Kettering-Toton with iron ore tipplers
1967	22nd August	2750hp Co-Co D1825, Derby-Wigston-Derby, loaded fly-ash wagons, riding test
	Unknown date	Static air-conditioning test with new MkII coaching stock

Further explanatory notes and background information

1952 – Testing of 4-6-2 70005 *John Milton*
The controlled road tests with 70005 *John Milton* in January and February 1952 are unique in that No 1 car was used in conjunction with MTUs 2 and 3, these being operated manually from within each vehicle.

1955 – Testing of "Fell" diesel-mechanical locomotive
The 2000hp 4-8-4 "Fell" diesel-mechanical was powered by four Paxman engines of 500hp each and had been under development by BR and Lt-Col LFR Fell at Derby since 1948. Two engines were situated in each nose in front of the two cab positions, and both pairs drove each of the two central axles, although all driving wheels were coupled as in normal steam practice. Designated 10100 by BR, the loco emerged from Derby Works in January 1951 and was engaged primarily on St Pancras-Manchester turns. It was purchased by BR in 1955 and tested on the Settle & Carlisle line, after which it was again put to work on the Midland

main line. Unfortunately it was seriously damaged in 1958 when its train-heating boiler caught fire in Manchester (Central) station, and it never returned to traffic. It was broken up in 1960.

Use after withdrawal by BR

Withdrawn from service in November 1970, No 1 car was stored in the sidings of the Railway Technical Centre at Derby, awaiting disposal. A private initiative rescued the vehicle from oblivion by its inclusion in Derby Museum's Midland Railway Project.

On 4th March 1971, it left the RTC for transfer to Derby Corporation's own sidings, where other items of rolling stock were already stored, pending ultimate transfer to the chosen museum site. This took place on 8th September 1975 when a trainload of 23 historic items were towed away, first to Toton sorting sidings and then in two groups to the selected Midland Railway Centre at Butterley the following week. After initial conservation and restoration work, the vehicle was on display over Easter 1978, but even by the year 2000 it had not yet reached the Midland Railway Trust's list of items for full restoration.

Consequently, the Princess Royal Class Locomotive Trust agreed to take on the task of transforming M45050 to first class condition. Ownership was transferred in September 2005, and a Heritage Lottery Grant was applied for and approved in March 2008, after which a contract was awarded to Rampart Carriage & Wagon Services Ltd back in Derby, to where movement took place on 14th May 2008. It was received back at Butterley on 23rd October of the same year

for final repainting into 1938 LMS crimson lake, and was outshopped on 28th January 2009.

To mark the project's completion, simulated test runs took place on 15th April 2009 when former dynamometer car personnel travelled in No 1 hauled by 6233 *Duchess of Sutherland* over the whole of the track available at Butterley. On the following day, other VIPs concerned with the project were afforded repeat runs. The vehicle now resides, on display, inside the Princess Royal Class Locomotive Trust's West Shed at the Butterley complex.

After being tested on the Rugby test plant in 1955, 4-6-2 46225 "Duchess of Gloucester" made follow-up road tests in May 1956 over the Settle & Carlisle route – nearly a year after the static tests had taken place. The main test load had been left at Skipton to enable 46225, No 3 dynamometer car and the three MTUs to run forward to turn, as one, on the Shipley triangle. After doing this, the train is seen heading north again between Saltaire and Bingley.
(R Butterfield/Initial Photographics)

Chapter 9

LMS/LMR No 3 Dynamometer Car

For details of LMS/LMR No 3 dynamometer car, see chapter 7 on page 39.

1949	22nd and 25th April	Running-in trials, Derby-Nottingham-Leicester-Derby

1949 — 22nd and 25th April — Running-in trials, Derby-Nottingham-Leicester-Derby

5th and 7th May — 4-6-0 45372, Rugby-Peterborough and return with MTUs 1, 2 and 3

9th May — 4-6-0 45578 *United Provinces*, Rugby-Willesden and return with MTUs 1 and 3. These first three runs were for testing the equipment and acquainting personnel with it.

10th May — 4-6-0 44752, Rugby-Manchester (London Road)

13th May — 4-6-0 45699 *Galatea*, Manchester (Central)-Derby with MTUs 1 and 2. After visiting the Rugby test plant, these two runs were special demonstration runs for the Institution of Locomotive Engineers' summer meeting, 10th to 13th May.

9th to 18th August — 4-6-0 44764, Derby-Willesden and return with MTUs 2 and 3 and corridor tender for coal and water tests (some with MTU 3, only)

1950 — 3rd March — 2-4-2T 10897, Rugby-Peterborough and return with MTUs 1, 2 and 3, tests with self-weighing grate

8th March — 4-6-2 35005 *Canadian Pacific*, Rugby-Willesden and return with MTUs 2 and 3

10th March — 45532 *Illustrious*, Rugby-Willesden and return with MTUs 2 and 3 piloting 4-4-0 41090, and 4-6-0 45672 *Anson* piloting 41090 on return run

16th March — 4-6-2 35005 *Canadian Pacific*, Rugby-Willesden-Stewarts Lane with MTUs 1, 2 and 3

22nd to 31st March — 4-6-2 35005 *Canadian Pacific*, Clapham Junction-Salisbury and return with MTUs 2 and 3, tests with Berkley mechanical stoker. MTUs 1, 2 and 3 used on 29th, MTUs 1 and 2 used on 30th.

18th April to 17th May — 4-6-2 35005 *Canadian Pacific*, Clapham Junction-Salisbury and return with MTUs 2 and 3, tests with hand-firing

7th, 12th and 26th September — Unknown locomotive, Derby-Chinley-Derby

10th October — Unknown locomotive, calibration runs with No 1 dynamometer car

21st November to 12th December — 4-6-0 44764, Willesden-Stafford and Oxford-Willesden, with corridor tender. MTUs 1, 2 and 3 used singly.

1951 — 13th March to 5th May — B1 4-6-0s 61370 and 61373, Peterborough-Grimsby and return with MTUs 2 and 3, wind resistance and fuel economy tests

10th May to 12th June — B1 4-6-0s 61370 and 61373, March-Norwich and return with MTUs 1, 2 and 3, repeat tests (61049 and 61970 also used)

18th to 29th June — Co-Co 750V DC electric 20003, Victoria-Newhaven and return (passenger) and Norwood-Horsham and return (freight)

2nd December — 4-6-0s 44667 and 45342, Toton-Brent, coal train test (loaded)

9th December — 4-6-0 45285, Brent-Toton, coal train test

12th December — Unknown locomotive, Derby-Chinley-Derby, calibration tests with No 1 dynamometer car

1952 — 6th January — 4-6-0s 44667 and 45342, repeat of 2nd December test

13th January — 4-6-0 45285, repeat of 9th December test

24th March to 7th May — WD 2-8-0 90464, Carlisle-Hurlford and return with MTUs 1 and 2 and corridor tender, controlled road tests at constant speeds for Bulletin 7

1952 continued	28th May to 9th July	WD 2-10-0 90772, Carlisle-Hurlford and return with MTUs 1, 2 and 3 used singly, in pairs or all three together with corridor tender, controlled road tests at constant speeds for Bulletin 7
	29th October	4-4-0 40934, Derby-Wath Central, positioning move with No 3 dynamometer car and MTUs 1, 2 and 3
	3rd to 14th November	EM1 Bo-Bo 1500V DC electrics 26030 and 26034, Wath-Dunford Bridge and return, coal trains with MTUs 1 or 3 singly, or 1, 2 and 3 all together
	17th to 26th November	EM1 Bo-Bo 1500V DC electrics 26030 and 26034, Wath-Dunford Bridge and return, further tests made in conjunction with the new ER dynamometer car and locomotives at each end, giving typical coal train formation of 26030, No 3 car, MTU, train, ER car, 26034
	1st to 3rd December	EM1 Bo-Bo 1500V DC electric 26030 used solo with plus No 3 dynamometer car and MTUs 1, 2 and 3
1953	13th to 27th October	4F 0-6-0 44203, Crewe-Holyhead and return with MTUs 1 and 2, testing "Swirlyflo" boiler tubes at constant steam rate
	3rd to 25th November	4F 0-6-0 44030, Crewe-Holyhead and return with MTU 1 only
	1st to 11th December	4F 0-6-0 44203, Crewe-Holyhead and return with MTUs 1 and 2
	15th December	4F 0-6-0 44030, Crewe-Derby, calibration test, formation: 44030, No 1 car, No 3 car, MTU 1, MTU 2, stores van

The corridor tender accompanied both WD locos on tests between Carlisle and Hurlford, and is seen here at Dumfries on 6th June 1952 paired with 2-10-0 90772 at the head of the No 3 dynamometer car, all three MTUs and a coal van. Although still lettered LMS here (and in red livery), the tender did later acquire BR black livery and the lion and wheel emblem. (Patrick Webb)

| 1954 | 12th to 20th January | 4F 0-6-0 44030, Crewe-Holyhead and return with MTUs 1 and 2, locomotive with modified front end. Car mileage: 24,322 from new, reset to read zero. |

1954   12th to 20th January   4F 0-6-0 44030, Crewe-Holyhead and return with MTUs 1 and 2, locomotive with modified front end. Car mileage: 24,322 from new, reset to read zero.

23rd March to 1st May   4-6-0 44981, Carlisle-Hurlford and return with MTUs 1, 2 and 3 used singly or in pairs with corridor tender

4th to 7th May   4-6-0 44987, repeat tests, car kept at Carlisle, locomotive coupled to corridor tender, coal and water tests with locomotives in various conditions

11th to 14th May   4-6-0 44988 repeat tests as above

18th to 21st May   4-6-0 44985 repeat tests as above

24th to 28th May   4-6-0 44964 repeat tests as above

31st May to 2nd June   4-6-0 44981 repeat tests as above

28th September to 22nd October   9F 2-10-0 92013, Carlisle-Skipton and return with MTUs 1, 2 and 3 used singly, in pairs or all three together for controlled road tests after tests at the Rugby test plant for Bulletin 13

6th to 10th December   4-6-0 44761, Carlisle-Skipton and return with MTUs 1, 2 and 3 used singly or in pairs. Up to 4 DMU motor cars (MC) and 4 driving trailer cars (DT) deployed for resistance tests for DMU stock. Example formation varied from MC, No 3 car, 44761, MTU 1 seen on 6th December to the astonishing sight of 44761, MTU 3, MTU 2, No 3 car, MC, DT, DT, MC, MC, DT, DT, MC on 10th December.

Prior to the opening (in 1954) of the Manchester-Sheffield-Wath 1500V DC electrification scheme, tests were carried out with the EM1 Bo-Bos between Wath and Dunford Bridge. At Wath on 25th November, 1952 one of the MTUs is nearest the camera, with 26035 alongside – not a loco actively used on the tests, which were with 26030 and 26034. (Patrick Webb)

1955	31st January	4-6-0 45052, Lichfield-Erdington, special 10-coach train at the request of the Chief Inspecting Officer of Railways following the Sutton Coldfield accident on 23rd January
	7th to 10th February	9F 2-10-0 92009, Toton-Brent and return, 800-900 ton coal train
	14th to 17th February	9F 2-10-0 92018, repeat tests
	6th March	4-6-0 44776, Bromsgrove-Blackwell, Lickey incline, stop/start tests with 7 coaches
	13th March	4-6-0 45554 *Ontario*, Bromsgrove-Blackwell, Lickey incline, stop/start tests with 8 coaches
	25th April to 19th May	2000hp 4-8-4 10100, "Fell" diesel mechanical, Carlisle-Skipton and return with MTUs 1, 2 and 3 all together or in pairs, controlled road tests. (12th May – see entry for No 1 car on page 44, no MTUs.)
	24th May	4-6-0 45094, Lichfield-Birmingham New Street
	5th to 7th September	4-6-0 45626 *Seychelles*, Derby-Leicester and return with MTU 2
	8th to 15th September	4-6-0 45610 *Gold Coast*, repeat tests and 4-6-0 45506 *The Royal Pioneer Corps*, repeat tests. Car mileage; 16,190 since 20th January 1954, reset to read zero
	11th October to 10th November	9F 2-10-0 92023 (Crosti boiler), Carlisle-Hurlford and return with MTUs 1, 2 and 3 used singly, in pairs or all together, controlled road tests after running on the Rugby plant
	22nd November to 9th December	9F 2-10-0 92050, repeat tests as for 92023 for Bulletin 13 (which covered 92013 and 92050 only)
	14th December	4-6-0 46120 *Royal Inniskilling Fusilier*, Manchester-Buxton and return
1956	20th March to 4th May	4-6-2 46225 *Duchess of Gloucester*, Carlisle-Skipton and return with MTUs 1, 2 and 3 all together or 2 and 3 as a pair, controlled road tests after running on the Rugby plant in 1955. 1st May only, maximum load test with No 3 car, MTU 2, van and 17 coaches amounting to 640 tons.
	20th August to 27th September	3300hp Co-Co *Deltic*, Carlisle-Skipton and return with MTUs 1, 2 and 3, performance and efficiency tests for Bulletin 19. (27th/28th August runs included the ER dynamometer car as well, coupled between the engine and No 3 car. 13th September, maximum load test with No 3 car and 19 coaches amounting to 643 tons.)
1957	24th January	4-6-0 46138 *The London Irish Rifleman*, Crewe-Carlisle, positioning move on the 12.30pm parcels
	29th to 31st January	Prototype Rolls Royce-engined DMU power car E50000, Carlisle-Skipton and return, solo then with 1 or 2 trailer cars
	18th to 20th September	DMU power car with two Rolls Royce engines M50136, Carlisle-Skipton and return, solo or with a trailer car
	1st to 22nd October	Longmoor Military Railway WD 2-10-0 601, Carlisle-Hurlford and return with MTU 1, or as a pair with MTU 2, performance and braking tests. Car mileage: 18,223 since 15th September 1955, reset to read zero.
	23rd, 24th October	WD 2-10-0 90763, Carlisle-Gretna Green and Dumfries-Carlisle, stopping distance tests
	22nd to 29th November	Longmoor Military Railway WD 2-10-0 601, Carlisle-Hurlford and return with MTUs 1 and 2, performance and braking tests, now as an oil-burner
	13th December	Unknown locomotive, Carlisle-Crewe for stabling in the paintshop
1958	16th January	Unknown locomotive, Crewe-Derby for repair in the works
	19th June	4-6-0 44861, Derby-Knighton South Junction and return with MTU 1, equipment check after works attention

LMS/LMR NO 3 DYNAMOMETER CAR

1958 continued	15th July to 10th September	1000hp Bo-Bo D8000, Toton-Rugby and return with MTUs 1 and 2 singly or as pair, performance and efficiency tests for Bulletin 11
	29th September	0-6-0 shunter D3573, Marylebone goods yard, container transfer system under test
	1st, 2nd, 5th and 26th October	1200hp Co-Bo D5700 and D5701, Hendon-Gushetfaulds and Chaddesden-Bedford and return, freight trials
	14th November to 17th December	800hp Bo-Bo D8208, Toton-Rugby (or Buxton or Edale) and return with MTU 1 and 2, performance and efficiency tests for Bulletin 12
1959	6th to 15th April	4-6-0 44920, Cheadle Heath-Rowsley and return, freight timings
	6th May to 9th July	1600hp Bo-Bo D5008, Toton-Rugby (or Buxton or Edale) and return with MTU 1 and 2, performance and efficiency tests for Bulletin 21. (On the runs of 30th June and 1st July No 3 car was paired with No 1 car on a 15-coach train.)
	14th to 16th September	0-6-0 shunter D3576, Toton yard with MTU 1, slow speed tests – ¾ mph on 50 16-ton wagons with different buffers
	6th to 9th October	2000hp 1Co-Co1 10203, Crewe-Carlisle and return with MTUs 2 and 3, wheelslip tests
	25th to 27th November	2552hp DC Bo-Bo E5009, Victoria-Dover-Stewarts Lane, wheelslip tests for Southern Region. Simulated "Night Ferry" load of 695 tons. Ten loaded hopper wagons between two brake vans.
1960	18th to 22nd January	2300hp 1Co-Co1 D8 *Penyghent*, Derby-Chinley-Leicester-Derby with MTUs 1, 2 and 3, flashover tests
	15th February to 24th March	2300hp 1Co-Co1 D8 *Penyghent*, Derby-Manchester- Derby with MTUs 1, 2 and 3
	24th June to 1st July	3200hp Bo-Bo E3003, East Didsbury-Wilmslow-Mauldeth Road and return with MTUs 1 and 3, and ex-gas turbine, E2001, by now crew training vehicle
	19th to 21st September	179hp 0-4-0 D2850, Treeton Junction-Beighton Junction with MTU 1, acceptance and performance tests
	18th, 19th October	2000hp 1Co-Co1 D296, Crewe-Shrewsbury and return, braking tests
1961	26th March to 16th April	2500hp 1Co-Co1 D16 and 2000hp 1Co-Co1 D230 *Scythia*, Derby-Luton and return, braking tests with a 15-coach train
	1st to 5th May	2000hp 1Co-Co1 D304, Derby-Manchester and return with MTUs 1, 2 and 3, performance and traction motor heating tests
	8th to 12th May	2000hp 1Co-Co1 D304, Derby-Brent and return, freight trials
	28th August to 1st September	204hp 0-6-0 D2512, Stourton Junction-Waterloo Colliery with MTU 1, performance and efficiency tests
	14th to 21st November	2000hp 1Co-Co1 D345 and 3300hp Bo-Bos E3047, E3033, E3010 and E3062, Crewe electric traction depot, handbrake tests on individual locomotives
	28th November to 7th December	2000hp 1Co-Co1 D211 *Mauretania*, Derby-Leicester and return with MTUs 1, 2 and 3, traction motor heating tests. Car mileage from 22nd October 1957 to 30th November 1961: 21,156 miles, reset to read zero.
	14th December	2750hp 4-6-0 gas turbine GT3, Crewe-Carlisle and return, performance tests
1962	6th, 7th and 13th May	3300hp Bo-Bo E3039, Crewe-Speke Junction and return with MTUs 2 and 3, traction motor heating tests
	21st May	2500hp 1Co-Co1 D150, Derby-Rowsley-Cheadle, formation: D150, brake tender, No 3 car, MTU 1, 28 wagons, van
	3rd June	2500hp 1Co-Co1 D150, Derby-Luton-Derby on 14 coaches, stopping distance tests

Car now stored at Horninglow between test runs, rather than Derby

1962 continued	8th to 10th August	3300hp Bo-Bo E3071, Wilmslow-Heald Green with MTUs 1, 2 and 3 together with Mobile Research Car DM 395001, motor suspension tests. Formation: E3071, DM395001, No 3 car, MTU 2, MTU 3, MTU 1, E3061, E3056.
	11th to 14th September	3300hp Bo-Bo E3087, repeat tests. Formation: E3087, DM395001, E3071, No 3 car, MTU 1, MTU 3, MTU 2, E3061, E3067.
	26th September	2500hp 1Co-Co1 D148, Wellingborough-Eaglescliffe, special load test with 38 iron ore tippler wagons
	16th to 19th October	3300hp Bo-Bo E3030, repeat tests. Formation: E3030, DM395001, E3071, No 3 car, MTU 1, MTU 3, E3087, E3060, E3072.
1963	20th to 23rd March	3300hp Bo-Bo E3100, Wilmslow-Sandbach with MTUs 1 and 2, adhesion tests on notchless control loco. Formation: E3100, No 3 car, MTU 1, MTU 2, E3067 and E3071 for rheostatic braking.
	26th March	3300hp Bo-Bo E3036, Wilmslow-Sandbach with MTUs 1 and 3. Formation: E3036, No 3 car, MTU 1, MTU 3, E3067, 2 Mk I coaches, E3071, Mk I coach.
	27th, 28th March	3300hp Bo-Bo E3036, Crewe-Liverpool-Stafford-Crewe with MTUs 1 and 3, load tests
	7th, 8th April	2500hp 1Co-Co1 D108, Wigston-Brent-Derby, special loads: 68 vans empty, then 10 full and 38 empty
	30th April to 24th May	3300hp Bo-Bo E3100, Crewe-Stafford and return with MTUs 1 and 3, adhesion tests. Formation: E3100, No 3 car, E3075, 2 Mk I coaches, E3087, Mk I, E3073.
	17th July	2500hp 1Co-Co1 D89, Wellingborough-Eaglescliffe, special load test with 47 iron-ore tippler wagons
	17th September to 10th October	1350hp Bo-Bo D6123, Carlisle-Hurlford and return with MTUs 1 and 3, performance and efficiency test with re-engined locomotive
	22nd December	2500hp 1Co-Co1 D140, Derby-Luton and return, stopping distance tests
1964	7th to 22nd April	3300hp Bo-Bos E3096, E3015 and E3093, Nuneaton-Lichfield (TV) with MTUs 2 and 3, resistance tests, European ferry wagons
	5th, 6th May	2500hp 1Co-Co1 D51, repeat of above tests
	10th, 11th June	2500hp 1Co-Co1 D45, Derby-Saffron Lane and return with MTUs 2 and 3, cab ventilation tests
	22nd, 23rd June	2750hp Co-Co D1745, Derby-Chinley-Millers Dale and return with MTUs 2 and 3, static field diversion tests
	9th, 10th December	2750hp Co-Co D1792, repeat of above tests
1965	18th February, 27th May and 2nd June	2750hp Co-Co D1820, Derby-Bedford and return, riding tests with 15 empty Freightliner wagons. Formation: D1820, 5 coaches, No 3 car, match wagon, Freightliner vehicles, match wagon, van. After these tests, No 3 car derailed at Derby and was shopped for new axles and wheel turning.
	16th to 18th June	1250hp Bo-Bo D7539, Derby-Bedford-Kettering and return with MTUs 1, 2 and 3, cab noise level tests. Formation: D7539, 8 coaches, No 3 car, MTU 1, MTU 2, MTU 3.
	23rd to 25th June	1250hp Bo-Bo D7542, repeat of above tests. Formation: D7542, 9 coaches, MTU 1, MTU 2, MTU 3, No 3 car.
	26th, 27th July	2750hp Co-Co D1830, Derby-Brent-Bedford-Derby, lateral movement of Freightliner wagons. Formation: D1830, 5 coaches, No 3 car, match wagon, Freightliners, match wagon, BSK.

1965 continued	13th to 16th September	2500hp 1Co-Co1 D138 and D154, Derby-Kettering-Derby with MTUs 1, 2 and 3, cab noise level tests
	11th, 12th November	3300hp Bo-Bo E3027, 2000hp 1Co-Co1 D233, 1550hp Bo-Bo D6550, 21.50 Northampton-Fawley oil train, mileage dispute checks (Esso/BR)
	13th, 14th November	1550hp Bo-Bo D6523, 22.10 Fawley-Northampton oil train, as above
	16th November	1550hp Bo-Bo D6585 and D6508, 07.40 Bromford Bridge-Fawley oil train, as above
	16th, 17th November	1550hp Bo-Bo D6569 and D6512, 22.55 Fawley-Bromford Bridge oil train, as above
1966	30th January	2750hp Co-Co D1832, Derby-Bedford and return, stopping distances with Freightliner vehicles
	2nd, 3rd March	2500hp 1Co-Co1 D37, Hendon-Gushetfaulds and return, riding tests with container wagons
	3rd, 4th March	2500hp 1Co-Co1 D11, repeat of above tests
	23rd to 28th March	3300hp Bo-Bo E3145, E3002, E3090 and E3196, Crewe-Rugby and return, riding tests with Pullman M550
	30th March	3300hp Bo-Bo E3126, Euston-Bletchley and return, wheel balancing tests on coaching stock. Formation: E3126, FK, SK, No 3 car, SO, SLS.
1966-1967		A series of similar tests continued to take place over this period, involving riding tests, driving cab ventilation and noise levels, disc-brake heating, carriage heating, braking distance tests, and so on. These were conducted on a variety of routes with various diesel and electric locomotives, and during 1967, all testing vehicles (from all regions) were centralised to work from the Railway Technical Centre, Derby.
1968	30th January to 23rd February	1750hp Co-Co D6700, Doncaster-Peterborough and return, braking and riding tests with a 9-coach push/pull set
	27th August to 25th September	Hawker Siddeley 4000 *Kestrel*, Derby-Crewe-Nuneaton-Leicester and return, performance and efficiency tests. Example formation: HS 4000, No 3 car, MTU 3, E3132 on 20th September.

Further explanatory notes and background information

The Berkley Mechanical Stoker
This was fitted at Eastleigh Works in April 1948, when *Canadian Pacific* had its number changed from 21C5 to 35005. The engine then underwent assessment trials on BR (SR) during 1948/9 before being sent to Rugby Locomotive Testing Station in March 1950 (although it was not tested there). It returned to Stewarts Lane in the company of dynamometer car No 3 and all three MTUs, to begin test runs to Salisbury and back in both stoker-fired and hand-fired modes. The stoker was finally removed in April 1951. The use of mechanical stokers on BR was restricted to this locomotive and, later, to three 9F 2-10-0s (92165/6/7) though here again the experiment was not long-lasting, use being confined to the years 1958-62 only.

The self-weighing grate
On the tests with both WD locos, 2-8-0 90464 and 2-10-0 90772, an experimental self-weighing fire grate was used.

When carrying out a controlled road test, one of the difficulties was to assess accurately the locomotive's coal consumption during the test run. If the amount of coal in the firebox at the start and finish of the test run was different, the difference had to be incorporated into the test data. While an experienced fireman would attempt to make the two states equal it was, at best, guesswork as to whether they were even roughly the same.

The self-weighing grate had been in development for a couple of years at this time, and was given trial fittings on the L&YR 2-4-2T 10897 (which belonged to the Testing Department) in conjunction with the No 3 car. The grate had sensors sufficiently sensitive to detect the weight of each additional shovelful of coal, and continuous readings were electrically transmitted to the dynamometer car, as well as being able to give the static weight of fire before and after the tests. Although this device was now working satisfactorily, no further tests (on any engine) made use of it.

Coal train tests
These appear to have begun between 15th and 18th November 1951 using a pair of spotless "Royal Scots" 46117 *Welsh*

Above: Air-braked 4-6-2 "Britannias" 70043 and 70044 pair up to conduct a fully-fitted coal train test between Toton and Brent on 28th November 1954, photographed at Kettering with a load of 70 wagons (1,556 tons) behind the recording car. Both engines were allocated to Longsight (9A) at the time, but were on loan to Toton (18A) for the duration of the tests. *(Patrick Webb)*

Below: This time, a brace of vacuum-braked 7MTs heads another coal train test, again at Kettering. The chosen pair, 70023 "Venus" and 70020 "Mercury", were of considerable interest being Old Oak Common (81A) engines, and went to Toton complete with WR-pattern lamps, as LMR lamps were incompatible with WR lamp brackets! The recording vehicle appears to be different from the one in the previous photograph. *(Alan Rimmer)*

Guardsman and 46154 *The Hussar* to double-head a 66-wagon (vacuum) fitted train. They were probably the first of a long series of tests spread over several years, and covered the running of the regular Toton-Brent coal trains. The tests involved comparing the operation of 16-ton mineral wagons fitted with either vacuum brakes or Westinghouse air brakes.

Test trains generally consisted of 50 loaded wagons if a pair of class 5s was used, or 70 loads if a pair of "Britannias" was employed. For the air-braked trials, the only locomotives used were the specially-equipped standard 4-6-0s 73030/1 or the 4-6-2s 70043/4, though a pair of L1 2-6-4Ts 67729/37 was also tried. Sometimes engines would be used singly with reduced loads. The same arrangements also applied with respect to the vacuum braked trains, and 73019 (14B Kentish Town) was seen on 2nd November 1952 conducting a Brent-Toton run with a formation of Recording Car, 52 wagons plus brake van. When double-headed, 73000/1 and 70020 *Mercury* + 70023 *Venus* were the usual pairs, and 70030 *William Wordsworth* if working solo. (There was special interest in the use of 70020/3, as these were WR-based engines at the time, allocated to 81A Old Oak Common!)

Later vacuum-braked trials involved pairs of 9F 2-10-0s, for example, 92153/6 in March/April 1959. It seems that only some runs had the services of a full dynamometer car. If not, the Recording Car M279496 belonging to the Carriage &

Wagon Engineer's Department had to suffice, or sometimes there would be no test vehicle at all, although the radio-fitted brake van E246726 was often employed on vacuum brake tests, and Westinghouse-fitted brake van 731181 on air brake tests. Similar tests continued to 1962 at least, with diesels.

Historical notes: the LMS/LMR No 3 car (M45049) after withdrawal

This car was finally taken out of service by BR in 1975 having covered an estimated 147,616 miles during its lifetime. Ownership was transferred from BR to the National Railway Museum on 23rd September 1977, the car being inscribed Test Car No 3 at the handover. The vehicle was then repainted externally commencing in October 1978, the livery changing from orange and blue to LMS maroon and now relabelled Dynamometer Car No 3. The running gear was also overhauled by BREL Carriage Works at York, and it was then exhibited at the Rocket 150 celebrations at Rainhill in 1980. The original intention during the 1980s was to restore the car to working order, but financial constraints reduced this to "display-only" status.

More recently, No 3 car has been loaned to the East Lancashire Railway at Bury between April 1994 and April

The interior of LMS/LMR dynamometer car No 3, photographed on 8th September 2001 during its time on display at Barrow Hill roundhouse. (Kestrel Collection)

1997, during which period all asbestos was removed from the vehicle. After this, a further loan agreement took it to the Barrow Hill roundhouse, where it arrived in November 1998. After cosmetic restoration there, it was moved in June 2011 to the Midland Railway Centre at Butterley where it is intended to be restored.

Historical notes: Mobile Test Unit 1 (M45053) after withdrawal

All three of the MTUs were transferred to Derby in 1967 at the same time as the various dynamometer cars were centralised there. During 1969, these MTUs were designated as Brake Units 1, 2 and 3 and continued in BR service until 1974. By 1976, all three were stabled out of use at Crewe Electric Traction Depot. Of the three, No 1 was in best condition, was nearest to being in original state and had seen least use in recent years. It was therefore this vehicle that was claimed by the NRM under the terms of the 1968 Transport Act. The two remaining brake units were later scrapped, but not until at least 1980.

Consequently Brake Unit No 1 (now ADM 45053M) was acquired by the NRM in 1978, but it received no attention until going to Litchurch Lane Carriage Works in 1981. Exactly what work was done here (if any) is unknown. Initially the idea was to have it overhauled by 1985, though in the end only "static display" was agreed, and the vehicle was returned to the NRM from Derby in December 1984. It was photographed in the South Yard at York in April 1990, still in orange and blue livery and lettered ADM 45053M, but apparently intact and in a reasonable external state.

At the time of writing, this historic unit still resides in the South Yard, although its condition has deteriorated markedly over the last 20 years, during which it appears to have not been touched. Its future (if it has one) is unknown.

North Eastern Railway 1100hp 1500V DC Bo-Bo electric locomotive No 8 seen on trial at Newport on 12th October 1921 with the NER dynamometer car. (National Railway Museum/SSPL)

Chapter 10

NER/LNER Dynamometer Car

This vehicle was constructed at York Carriage & Wagon Works, fitted out at Gateshead Works, and entered service in 1906. The car was built following the loan (in 1903/4) by the GWR of its own dynamometer car and drawings for certain parts. The NER vehicle therefore closely matched the GWR car in its design and fittings, and was also equipped with a spring dynamometer. Given the running number 3591 by the NER, it was stored when not in use at Stooperdale wagon repair shops within the Darlington Works complex.

Pre-grouping use, significant runs only, 1906-1922

1906	6th to 8th March	4-4-0 2109, 3.32pm Newcastle-Edinburgh via NBR into Scotland with ECJS coaches. 11.15pm return. (The car's first run.)
1907	January/February	4-4-2 713, York-Newcastle and return, electric lighting trials
1908	March/April	4-4-2 1235, Newcastle-Edinburgh and return, superheater trials
1909	18th, 19th February	Unknown locomotive, Royal Train – Doncaster-York-Newcastle-Edinburgh via GNR, NER and NBR companies
	11th May	Newcastle-Tynemouth, 3-car electric set and steam autocar, acceleration comparison tests
1912	11th February	Bo-Bo electric locomotive No 2, Heaton shed-Heaton East
1914	February	Unknown locomotive, GNR Lincoln-Boston, engine pull tests
1916	2nd April	Bo-Bo electric locomotive No 6, acceptance trials
1921	12th October	Bo-Bo electric locomotive No 8, maximum power tests (see photograph opposite)
1922	22nd to 28th May	GNR 1000 and GNR 1646, Peterborough-Boston, wagon resistance tests. GWR car No 7 also took part.
	4th June to 11th January 1923	Bo-Bo electric locomotives Nos 4, 6, 12 and 13, Shildon-Newport, performance tests. 19 runs between these dates. Maximum load of 1,400 tons handled.

Post-grouping LNER use, significant runs only, 1923-1939

The car was renumbered from 3591 to 23591 and then 902502 during this period.

1923	April/May	4-6-2 2400, Newcastle-Edinburgh and return
	25th June to 4th July	4-6-2 1472 *Flying Scotsman* and 4-6-2 2400, Doncaster-King's Cross and return, comparative trials between NER and GNR Pacific designs
1925	21st May	York (Layerthorpe)-Cliffe Common, steam Sentinel test on the Derwent Valley Light Railway
	6th September	2-8-2 2393, Peterborough-Ferme Park with 100 wagons
	1st to 12th December	0-6-0s 8280 and 8287, Stratford-Whitemoor, freight trials comparing Lentz and piston-valve gears
1926	28th June to 8th July	Various locomotives on train resistance tests between Manchester (London Road) and Sheffield (Victoria)
1927	16th and 30th October	SR 2-6-4T A803, Huntingdon-St Neots (16th October) SR 2-6-4T A890, Huntingdon-St Neots, oscillation tests SR 4-6-0 E782 *Sir Brian*, Woking-Walton (30th October)

1928	April to August	Car to York C&W Works for overhaul. Following the introduction of corridor tenders (in this year), the car was fitted with a vestibule connection at the front end to enable staff to pass through to the engine footplate. This forward-facing vestibule did not, however, have the usual concertina connection with the engine's corridor tender, but a special waterproof door was fitted beyond which was a (small) open space to stride over before entering the adjoining vestibule. This was necessary as there had to be no frictional resistance between the engine and the dynamometer car, as this would affect the dynamometer spring reading. (An earlier overhaul had provided a standard vestibule connection at the rear of the car to afford access to similarly-fitted passenger stock trailing the car.) GNR-type bogies were also fitted at this 1928 overhaul.
	24th September to 9th October	Kitson-Still steam/diesel 2-6-0, Darlington-Starbeck and return, trials with experimental locomotive
1929	4th to 14th February	251 *Derbyshire,* Leeds-Newcastle and return, trials with Kylala blastpipe versus standard blastpipe
	8th to 15th August	Kitson-Still steam/diesel 2-6-0, Darlington-Starbeck and return, oil and water consumption tests
1930	13th to 23rd February	4-6-4 10000, Darlington-King's Cross-Leeds-Edinburgh-Perth, trials with Gresley's experimental high-pressure 4-cylinder engine
1931	4th September	4-6-4 10000, maximum pull test at Shildon
	19th November	4-6-4 10000, Darlington-York, indicator tests
1933	9th April	4-6-0 5427, Leicester-Loughborough, brake tests 4-4-2 4412, Leicester-Loughborough, brake tests
	21st, 22nd June	Kitson-Still steam/diesel 2-6-0, York-Hull, performance tests
1934	19th June to 11th July	2-8-2 2001 *Cock o' the North*, King's Cross-Grantham-Doncaster and return, indicator tests (see photograph on page 2)
	22nd, 23rd August	4-6-4 10000 and 4-6-0 756, York-Darlington and return, tests with counter-pressure locomotive
	30th November	4-6-2 4472 *Flying Scotsman*, King's Cross-Leeds and return, 100mph achieved on up run
1935	5th March	4-6-2 2750 *Papyrus,* King's Cross-Newcastle and return, 108mph achieved on up run
	29th May to 7th July	4-6-4 10000 and 4-6-0 761 as counter-pressure locomotive, Leeds-Hull-Newcastle, tests with a double chimney on the 4-6-4
	27th September	4-6-2 2509 *Silver Link*, Doncaster-Peterborough and return, brake tests with "Silver Jubilee" stock, 112½mph achieved on up run
1936	23rd October	4-4-0 232 *The Badsworth* and 4-6-2 2507 *Singapore*, Newcastle-Edinburgh and return, brake trials with double-headed train
1936/7	14th December to 8th January	4-6-0 2861 *Sheffield Wednesday* and 4-6-0 761 as counter-pressure locomotive, Darlington-York, new indicating equipment tests
	20th to 22nd April	2-6-0 1388 and 4-6-0 761 as counter-pressure locomotive, Darlington-York, new indicating equipment tests
1938	15th to 17th March	4-6-0 2861 *Sheffield Wednesday* and 4-6-0 761 as counter-pressure locomotive, Darlington-York, new indicating equipment tests
	3rd July	4-6-2 4468 *Mallard*, King's Cross-Grantham and return, brake tests. World record 126mph reached on up run.

This was the last logged pre-war run. However, during 1939, the LNER was busy developing the cathode ray oscilloscope method of electronic indicating (with A4 Pacifics in mind), and trial runs were made to test this equipment. These concerned class A1 and A3 locos running from Newcastle to Edinburgh, and a K3 2-6-0 together with 4-6-0 1699 (ex-761) as counter-pressure locomotive) between Darlington and York.

Post-war LNER use, 1946/7

1946	30th May	2-6-2T 484 and 4-6-2T 1766, refamiliarisation runs
	29th October to 15th November	4-6-2 500 *Edward Thompson*, Newcastle-Leeds, coal, water consumption tests
	19th November to 6th December	2-6-2 959, Newcastle-Edinburgh, coal, water consumption tests
1947	June to October	Car overhauled at York C&W Works
	14th to 24th October	4-6-0 1607 *Blickling* and 4-6-0 1622 *Alnwick Castle* worked the 10.10am Norwich-Liverpool Street and 3.40pm return – 1607: 14th, 15th, 23rd, 24th; 1622: 16th, 17th, 21st, 22nd. Comparison trials between the 2-cyl B2 1607 and 3-cyl B17 1622

British railways use, 1948-1951

1948	20th to 25th January	Car to York C&W Works for repairs to vestibule, inspection of bogies and overhaul of batteries
	1st March	Calibrated at Darlington prior to the Interchange Trials (see Chapter 2)
	8th, 9th April	4-6-2 60112 *St. Simon*, 1.10pm King's Cross-Leeds and 7.50am return, preliminary runs
	20th April	4-6-2 60034 *Lord Faringdon*, King's Cross-Leeds, Interchange Trials – first run
	3rd September	2-8-0 63773, Bristol-Eastleigh, Interchange Trials – last run
1949	26th April to 20th May	4-6-2 60114 *W. P. Allen* and 60539 *Bronzino*, King's Cross-Leeds, comparative tests between A1 and A2 locomotives as neither class had featured in the Interchange Trials.
1950	20th March to 2nd May	4-6-2 60533 *Happy Knight*, 2-6-0 61810 and 2-6-0 61921, King's Cross-Doncaster, trials to standardise freight workings of ER, LMR and WR of the new BR
	10th July to 28th September	2-6-0s 31618 and 31630 and 0-6-6-0T 36001, Eastleigh-Woking, coal and water tests with "Leader" and conventional locomotives (see photograph on page 60)
1951	4th to 7th June	4-6-2 70006 *Robert Burns* and 4-6-0 61270, Liverpool Street-Norwich-Harwich, performance tests on new loco and comparison runs over the same routes
	2nd to 10th October	500hp 0-8-0 Hunslet diesel-mechanical shunter (a non-BR loco) performs trip working between Stourton Yard (Leeds), Guiseley and Yeadon, and also on Stourton- Lancaster freight trains. (See photograph on back cover.) These are the last recorded runs of this vehicle, now officially withdrawn from service, but which remains stored at Stooperdale, Darlington.

Further explanatory notes and background information

The Bulleid "Leader" class 0-6-6-0T
This unconventional design was put in hand in order to combat the noticeable deficiency in large passenger tank engines on the Southern Railway, and its development overlapped the transition to British Railways. It was also intended to be an advance on existing designs of tank engines by virtue of possessing the power of a light Pacific, and the double-ended driving positions of diesel or electric locomotives. This latter provision did however leave the fireman isolated in a small space amidships – a retrograde step.

It was powered by six cylinders, three driving each of the six-wheeled bogies. On each bogie the centre axle was the driving axle, and this was coupled by chains to the inner and outer axles, the chains being contained in an oil-bath, another weakness of the design.

The test runs listed were not successful enough to warrant further experimentation, and 36001 was scrapped soon afterwards, along with the four other semi-complete members of the class being built at Brighton. It had been the intention to name the engines after distinguished persons, hence the class title "Leader". If 36001 had entered service it would have been allocated the name *Sir Winston Churchill*.

Historical notes: the NER/LNER car (902502) after withdrawal

After its last test runs, 902502 returned to Darlington for storage at Stooperdale Paint Shop within the North Road Works complex, and was joined in December by its replacement 320041, newly built at Doncaster C&W Works. Both cars underwent periodic calibration tests together for the next few years, after which 902502 remained in storage, although some of its equipment had been donated to 320041.

However in February 1962 it came to the notice of the Curator of Historical Relics (Dr CRL Scholes) that the NER car was to be withdrawn. Estimates were therefore requested from Darlington as to what it would cost to put the vehicle into exhibition condition, for subsequent display in the Museum of British Transport at Clapham.

These estimates were duly obtained (total cost £435) and the work authorised. Darlington carried out the mechanical renovation in June 1963, and the car was then transferred to York C&W Works to begin the restoration of the coachwork and fittings, work commencing in July 1963.

Although at the end of November 1964 this work was not yet completed, Dr Scholes had in the meantime acquired space at Clapham for the car to be positioned behind *Mallard*, and had obtained approval for the movement expenditure by the BRB, provided it was within the 1964 budget. The car

therefore had to be moved more or less straight away. Consequently, the car left York on Wednesday 16th December 1964 in the 3.33am parcels train to King's Cross, and was moved round to Nine Elms depot, staying there until the 21st.

Having got as far as possible by rail, the last leg of the journey was by road, with Pickfords doing the honours, a task complicated by the necessity of separating the car body from its bogies, transporting them in two moves and re-uniting them on arrival. Some pipework, brake gear and the dynamo belt was replaced the following day and 902502, now restored to 1938 condition and paired with 4468 *Mallard* to simulate the record breaking run of 3rd July 1938, was finally established in its new location.

The outstanding work, unfinished on leaving York, was then completed on a voluntary basis throughout 1965. This was accomplished by Mr Peter Howe, who had a long association with the vehicle as a member of the testing team at Darlington, commuting at weekends from Darlington until the job was done. On a subsequent visit to Clapham by HRH the Duke of Edinburgh on 18th November 1969 Mr Howe was on hand, by invitation, to answer the Duke's many questions as to its operation.

With the establishment of the National Railway Museum at York, Clapham's exhibits were disbanded, and 902502 reversed its north-to-south move of 1964 to become one of the star attractions at the NRM, again positioned behind *Mallard*, as a pair. The car arrived in York a few months ahead of the actual opening, giving Mr Howe the opportunity to "spring clean" the car before relinquishing it into the hands of the new Curator Dr John Coiley, who had nothing but praise for the standard of its presentation. It remains an NRM exhibit to this day.

Chapter 11

LNER/BR Dynamometer Car

This car was ordered by the LNER, and was partially complete at the outbreak of the Second World War, but it was destroyed by fire at Doncaster Works in 1940. Work on its replacement commenced in 1949, the car being equipped with the recoding table and hydraulic dynamometer manufactured by Messrs Alfred Amsler for the original car, but supplied post-war at the astonishing cost of £5,437 12s 0d (1938 prices!) Between use, the car was nearly always kept at Stooperdale.

1951	13th December	New car completed at Doncaster Works as DE320041, and makes a trial run to Grantham and back
	19th December	Transfers to Stooperdale Paint Shop, Darlington
1952	20th February	Both new and old cars undergo calibration tests between Darlington and Barnard Castle
	21nd August	Further calibration tests with both cars, Croft Junction-Croft depot
	27th August to 3rd November	Darlington to Middleton-in-Teesdale and return, adjustments to new car (not every day during this period!)
	14th November	Moved to Wath on the 6.25am Darlington-Doncaster
	17th November to 5th December	1848hp DC Bo-Bo 26030 and 26034, Wath-Dunford Bridge-Wombwell, coal train tests operated jointly with the LMR No 3 dynamometer car
1953	5th February	Calibration run with both cars, Darlington-Leeds (City) and back
	17th March	Darlington to Doncaster for minor attention
	16th April	Returns to Darlington renumbered as DB999500
	7th, 8th May	Darlington-Neasden via Woodford Halse
	11th to 22nd May	2-6-4Ts 67771 and 67794, special trains Marylebone-Woodford Halse, tests on different cylinder sizes
	2nd July	4-6-2 70000 *Britannia*, Sheffield (Victoria)-Doncaster and return, demonstration run for the Institution of Mechanical Engineers' summer outing
	15th, 16th July	200hp 0-4-0 diesel-hydraulic shunter 11700, tests with representatives of North British Locomotive Co present. Maximum power test, Croft Junction sidings, then Darlington-Piercebridge special train.
	8th October	2-6-2T 67618 and 4-6-2T 69889, Darlington-Saltburn, dynamometer car equipment test. 4-6-2T on return run.
	12th November	J21 0-6-0, Croft branch, calibration test with NER car 902502
	18th November	2-6-4T 67717, Darlington-Saltburn, calibration test with NER car 902502
	25th to 27th November	204hp 0-6-0 diesel-mechanical shunter 11105, comparison test with 11700, Croft depot branch. Maximum power tests, then Darlington-Piercebridge.
1954	26th January to 2nd February	4-6-0 61017 *Bushbuck*, Leeds (City)-Hull, service trains, left-hand cylinder indicated
	9th to 11th August	200hp 0-4-0 diesel-hydraulic 11702, Darlington-Piercebridge with North British Locomotive Co staff present. Also on the Croft branch.

Opposite: *Apart from GT3, the most unconventional locomotive tested during the period 1948-68 was the Bulleid 0-6-6-0T 36001, which is described in the text. Seen here on 23rd August 1950, on the four-track section northbound out of Eastleigh heading for Guildford, 36001 has the former NER dynamometer car next to the engine leading a string of empty carriage stock of some vintage. (SC Townroe, courtesy RK Blencowe)*

1954 continued	28th September to 1st October	4-6-0 61035 *Pronghorn* and 61016 *Inyala*, Leeds (City)-Hull, service trains, riding tests with 60% and 36% driving wheel balancing
1955	4th, 5th January	204hp 0-6-0 diesel-mechanical 11105 and 200hp 0-4-0 diesel-hydraulic 11702, Croft Junction-Croft depot, acceleration tests 400 tons to 14mph from rest
	13th February	2470hp DC Co-Co 27004, Manchester (London Road)-Sheffield (Victoria), special passenger trains, performance tests with 380 tons
	20th February	2470hp DC Co-Co 27004, Dewsnap-Rotherwood sidings, special freight with 650-700 tons
	13th, 20th March	1848hp DC Bo-Bo 26052, repeat of tests with 27004
	11th August	4-6-0 45384, Tayport-Wormit (3 runs) following derailment at Wormit
	25th September	A1 60128 *Bongrace*, Grantham-Peterborough, brake tests on freight wagons with 17-inch and 18-inch vacuum
1956	17th January to 3rd February	350hp 0-6-0s 15001, 13156 and 13143, trials over the Grimsby-Immingham light railway, tractive effort and acceleration tests with empty and loaded wagons
	14th, 17th February	4-6-2 60133 *Pommern*, King's Cross-Peterborough, brake tests with ATC (Automatic Train Control) equipment on passenger and freight trains
	21st, 24th February	2-6-2 60821, repeat of test with 60133
	27th, 28th August	3300hp Co-Co *Deltic*, Carlisle-Skipton, calibration tests with old NER car, LMR No 3 car and MTUs
	18th September	Unknown locomotive, Darlington-Saltburn, calibration test with old NER car
	23rd October	Unknown locomotive, Darlington-Doncaster works and back
	25th November	4-6-2 60034 *Lord Faringdon*, King's Cross-Grantham, brake tests with ATC equipment
	4th, 7th, 11th and 13th December	350hp 0-6-0 13117, Darlington-Fighting Cocks/Barnard Castle, fuel consumption and tractive effort tests on yard transfer workings. Car mileage: 12,446 since new.
1957	2nd to 10th April	4-6-2 60055 *Woolwinder*, extra coach on "The Talisman" 4-6-2 60073 *St. Gatien*, extra coach on "The Tees-Tyne Pullman" 4-6-2 60060 *The Tetrarch*, extra coach on the 10.10am to Edinburgh 4-6-2 60054 *Prince of Wales*, extra coach on the 10.10am ex-Edinburgh (Locomotives not necessarily in this order)
	20th May to 14th August	210hp 0-6-0 Hudswell-Clark *Enterprise*, Darlington-Fighting Cocks branch (opposite), Newport yard (Tees-side), tractive effort and fuel consumption tests
	26th, 29th November	4-6-2 60136 *Alcazar*, Doncaster-King's Cross service trains, riding tests of A1 class locomotive. RH/LH then LH/middle cylinders indicated.
1958	27th, 28th February	1250hp A1A-A1A D5504, Doncaster carriage yards, exhauster tests with 7 and 14 coach trains
	21st April to 3rd May	350hp 0-6-0 Hunslet locomotive with "Hydromatic" transmission, Darlington-Fighting Cocks-Shildon, tractive effort and fuel consumption tests
	7th May	350hp 0-6-0s 12104 and 12135, Temple Mills yard, hump-shunting tests
	12th to 17th May	2-6-2 60821, ATC braking tests with slow speed freight trains
	19th May to 6th June	1250hp A1A-A1A D5506, ATC braking tests with slow speed freight trains
	18th, 19th June	350hp 0-6-0 Hunslet locomotive with "Hydromatic" transmission, Newport yard, hump-shunting tests
	July	To Doncaster for lifting. Car mileage: 18,626 reset to read zero.

Above: A non-BR 0-6-0 diesel shunter on test on the Fighting Cocks branch out of Darlington. The BR(ER) car, in carmine and cream, is sandwiched between the diesel and a WD 2-8-0 (presumably "dead" as extra weight) with a sizeable train of mineral wagons – quite a task for a small 210hp loco. Taken between May and August 1957. (Collection RN Redman)

Below: When introduced in 1955, the prototype "Deltic" began its trials on the LMR, but in 1958 switched to the ER. Despite their later renown as express passenger engines, their high tractive effort could be put to good use on freight trains if required. This, however, is a trial run with the BR(ER) dynamometer car and 50 loaded coal wagons, southbound at Potters Bar on 21st March 1959. (National Railway Museum/SSPL)

1958 continued	29th September to 7th October	4-6-0 61087, Doncaster-New England, resistance tests on express freight vehicles
	8th October	2-6-0 61887, Doncaster-New England, resistance tests on express freight vehicles
	9th, 10th October	2-10-0 92196, Doncaster-New England, resistance tests on express freight vehicles
	15th November to 9th December	1250hp A1A-A1A D5516, Temple Mills-Whitemoor and Stratford-Norwich, performance and efficiency tests for Bulletin 14
1959	5th to 21st March	3300hp Co-Co *Deltic*, King's Cross-Grantham, press run on 5th March. King's Cross-Leeds-Grantham-Newcastle, runs between 11th and 19th March (various dates). Doncaster-Ferme Park, freight on 21st March (photograph, page 63).
	7th to 19th April and 20th to 25th April	2000hp 1Co-Co1 D206, Grantham-Hornsey (passenger trains) and Grantham-Bottesford (freight trains), brake tests with ATC equipment
	23rd, 24th June	Drewry shunter, Darlington-Piercebridge-Winston, trip work tests
	27th June	Car to Doncaster for lifting
	6th to 8th October	2000hp 1Co-Co1 D206, Hornsey-Grantham, brake trials
	9th to 13th November	1600hp A1A-A1A D5545, Norwich-Stratford (passenger)
	17th, 18th November	1600hp A1A-A1A D5545, Temple Mills-March (freight)
	20th November	4-6-2 70053 *Moray Firth*, Stratford-Ipswich-Norwich, special high-speed brake trials with empty carriage stock, locomotive fitted with speedometer
	7th to 8th December	1365hp A1A-A1A D5565, Hornsey-New England, brake trials
	10th, 11th December	2000hp 1Co-Co1 D208 and 2-10-0 92188, Hornsey-New England, brake trials
1960	26th February	L1 2-6-4T, Darlington-Newcastle (via coast) and return via main line to calibrate Carriage and Wagon Department decelerometer
	29th to 31st March	2000hp 1Co-Co1 D201 and D248, King's Cross-Doncaster, time trials
	12th, 13th May	2000hp 1Co-Co1 D272, Newcastle-King's Cross, time trials with 47 wagons. King's Cross-Darlington, 13th May.
	20th, 21st July	3300hp Co-Co *Deltic*, Harringay-Grantham, brake trials
	4th to 7th October	1160hp Bo-Bo D5311, Doncaster-Scunthorpe, brake tests
	11th to 21st October	1365hp A1A-A1A D5654, Doncaster-Scunthorpe, brake tests
	24th November	0-8-0s 63424 and 63451, Newport-Haverton Hill, 1,509 tons maximum pull test (double-headed)
1961	24th to 27th January	2000hp 1Co-Co1 D209, High Dyke-Frodingham, timing trials
	31st January to 3rd February	2500hp 1Co-Co1 D13, High Dyke-Frodingham, timing trials
	4th February	2500hp 1Co-Co1 D13, Doncaster-New England, 14 coaches
	7th to 8th February	1365hp A1A-A1A D5682, Doncaster-Brocklesby, braking and timing trials
	9th to 13th February	2500hp 1Co-Co1 D13, Doncaster-Brocklesby, braking and timing trials
	10th February	2-8-0 63652, Doncaster-Brocklesby, braking and timing trials
	15th February	0-8-0s 63353 and 63446, Brandon Colliery-Haverton Hill, coal train trials, 1,316 tons (double-headed)
	21st February	1750hp Co-Co D6703, Liverpool Street-Norwich, time trials
	22nd to 24th February	1750hp Co-Co D6704, Whitemoor-March-Temple Milles, freight train brake trials
	3rd March	1365hp A1A-A1A D5587, Whitemoor-March-Temple Mills, freight train brake trials

1961 continued	7th March	2000hp 1Co-Co1 D203, Whitemoor-March-Temple Mills, freight train brake trials
	8th March	1365hp A1A-A1A D5583 and D5585, Whitemoor-March-Temple Mills freight train brake trials (double-headed)
	15th, 21st and 22nd March	3300hp Co-Co D9001, King's Cross-Doncaster-Newcastle and return, timing trials (see photograph below)
	11th April	1250hp Bo-Bo D5151, Darlington-Leeds-Newcastle-Darlington, timing trials (car to Grantham MPD
	18th to 28th April	1365hp A1A-A1A D5646, Grantham-Bottesford, braking tests (car to Doncaster MPD)
	2nd to 9th May	1365hp A1A-A1A D5646, Doncaster-Boston-Barkston-Doncaster, braking tests
	10th, 11th May	4-6-0 61121, Doncaster-Boston-Barkston-Doncaster, braking tests
	20th June	3300hp Co-Co D9003, Hornsey-Doncaster, power, braking trials
	10th July	Car to Doncaster for repairs, returned to Darlington, 18th August. Car mileage: 27,894 reset to read zero.
	30th August	1250hp Bo-Bo D5157 and D5154, Newport-Normanton and return, drawbar pull tests

During March 1961 "Deltic" D9001 (later named St. Paddy) undertook speed trials with the BR(ER) car between King's Cross and Newcastle. The train description 1Z25 indicates an express passenger (1), special working (Z), train number 25 in the working timetable. The ensemble is seen pausing briefly at Darlington South signalbox heading north.
(National Railway Museum/SSPL)

1961 continued	8th September	1250hp Bo-Bo D5151 and D5155, Newport-Skinningrove and return, drawbar pull tests
	24th, 26th October	2800hp Co-Co D0280 *Falcon*, freight timing trials around Doncaster
	15th, 16th November	2500hp 1Co-Co1 D25, Newcastle-King's Cross, timing trials
	5th, 6th December	2-10-0 92200, Doncaster-New England, freight timing trials
	7th, 8th December	2-8-0 90476, Doncaster-New England, freight timing trials
	12th, 13th December	2-6-2 60872 *King's Own Yorkshire Light Infantry*, Doncaster-New England, freight timing trials
	14th, 15th December	4-6-0 61145, Doncaster-New England, freight timing trials
1962	8th, 9th April	Unknown locomotive, hump shunting at Ripple Lane and Temple Mills
	25th, 26th April	2-8-0 48209, Doncaster-Brocklesby, braking and starting tests
	10th, 17th May	1365hp A1A-A1A D5695 and D5699, Stratford-Norwich, braking tests with "Roadrailers". (Car to Finsbury Park.)
	29th, 30th May	2000hp A1A-A1A D5835, King's Cross-Doncaster, timing trials
	31st May	1365hp A1A-A1A D5801, Goodmayes-Cambridge-Bury St Edmunds-Ipswich, "Roadrailer" tests
	4th June	2500hp 1Co-Co1 D106, Darlington-Newport, special load timing trials with 1,319 tons
	12th, 13th June	2000hp A1A-A1A D5835, Doncaster-King's Cross (passenger), timing trials
	14th, 15th June	2000hp A1A-A1A D5835, Doncaster-Brocklesby (freight), load trials
	10th October	3300hp Co-Co D9018 *Ballymoss*, King's Cross-Doncaster, timing trials
	11th October	2750hp Co-Co D1500, King's Cross-Doncaster, timing trials
	31st October to 7th November	2000hp A1A-A1A D5834 and 1750hp Co-Co D6754, Doncaster-Barnetby and back, tests with Dowty couplings 1750hp Co-Co D6754, Doncaster-King's Cross, brake trials
1963	3rd January	1250hp Bo-Bo D5176, Darlington-Newcastle and return, performance and efficiency test
	22nd January to 6th February	2750hp Co-Co D1505, Doncaster-Brocklesby, disc brake trials
	12th to 14th March	3300hp Co-Co D9012 *Crepello*, King's Cross-Leeds and back, train heating boiler tests
	23rd April to 1st May	3300hp Co-Co D9001 *St. Paddy*, Hornsey-Wood Green-Doncaster, high-speed braking trials
	2nd, 3rd May	2750hp Co-Co D1514, Hornsey-Doncaster and return, "Roadrailer" braking tests
	22nd May	2750hp Co-Co D1500, Enfield Chase-Doncaster-Ferme Park, "Roadrailer" braking tests
	11th June	1750hp Co-Co D6735, York-King's Cross, "Roadrailer" braking tests
	12th June	Car to Doncaster for lifting, returned to Darlington, 22nd June. Car mileage: 20,203 reset to read zero.
	28th June	1250hp Bo-Bo D5181, Darlington-Newcastle and return, power and performance tests
	14th August	1250hp Bo-Bo D5181, Darlington-Leeds-York-Darlington, power and performance tests
	8th to 25th October	1365hp A1A-A1A D5584, Colwick-Hartby-Bottesford-Colwick, brake trials with fully and partially fitted freights

1963 continued	5th to 7th November	2500hp 1Co-Co1 D207, Norwich-Colchester, braking trials
1964	2nd February	2750hp Co-Co D1514, Doncaster-Thorp March Power Station, load and braking tests with 1,414 tons
	9th February	2750hp Co-Co D1553, Doncaster-Scunthorpe, load and braking tests with 1,500 tons
	20th March	1365hp A1A-A1A D5677, King's Cross-Doncaster, braking tests
	15th to 29th April	3300hp Co-Co D9001 *St. Paddy*, Hornsey-Harringay-Doncaster, high speed braking tests
	7th September	2-8-0 90005, Worksop-Retford, load tests

Last logged run available – car mileage at this point: 7,241

Historical notes: the LNER/BR car (DB999500) subsequent to 1964

On 26th May 1967, DB999500 passed into the control of the Director of Design, Railway Technical Centre, Derby. During the latter months of the year it was fitted with electric train heating, making the car suitable for use on electrified lines.

In February 1968 the Westinghouse Air Brake system was installed and the car was designated TEST CAR 2, and painted in blue and red livery.

The car was severely damaged in a shunting accident at the RTC on 21st January 1974 and was subsequently scrapped.

Its place was taken by the converted Mk1 BSK ADB975397 which became a temporary test car between February 1974 and February 1976. This underwent conversion to test car standards, and was fully repainted at Litchurch Lane, Derby. It then entered service as TEST CAR 2 on 8th July 1976.

Further information

The last time a steam engine was indicated was in May 1958 when the purpose was to investigate the steam distribution in the cylinders of A1 class locomotives on BR(ER). To this end 60136 *Alcazar* was tested (with modified valve settings) and the middle and left-hand cylinders were indicated using Crosby indicators. Preliminary runs were made out and back between Doncaster and York on 1st May, with the main runs next day from Doncaster to King's Cross and return. Two men operated the equipment behind the shelter and no dynamometer car was required, the readouts being analysed back at Darlington (see photograph on page 24).

D1794 heads test train 4Z59 on 4th June 1965. The BR(ER) car is employed, and a long rake of loaded HAA hopper wagons trails the 2750hp Co-Co near Brocklesby. Note the absence of a guard's van by this time. (National Railway Museum/SSPL)

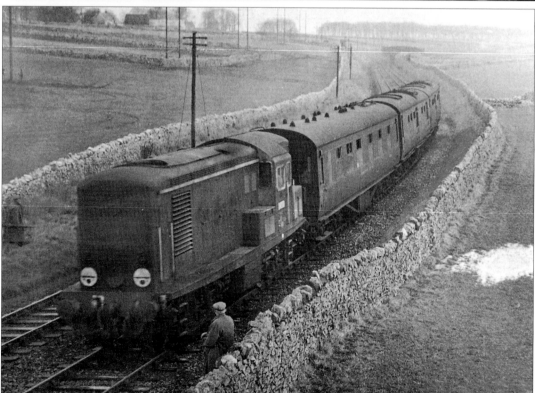

Above: *Contrasting freight trials on the ER! Seventeen years before the previous photo, the LMS No 1 car is seen behind a GWR 2-8-0 on the LNER main line during the Interchange Trials, on 25th August 1948.*
(National Railway Museum/SSPL)

Below: *During the period 14th November to 17th December 1958, D8208 is seen undergoing trials near Hindlow (on the Ashbourne-Buxton line) with the LMR No 3 car and MTUs 1 and 3 in tow. (ER Morten)*

Chapter 12

The Bulletins

The following paragraphs are each a brief synopsis of a document written up by the dynamometer car staff at the conclusion of a series of test runs. This document ("report") went before the Locomotive Testing Committee, and if found to be satisfactory (as it usually was) was then accepted, circulated within BR Departments and ultimately filed. Although reports were written at the end of every dynamometer car test, only those listed below, considered to be of particular relevance or importance, were given the title "Bulletin", and these were put on sale to the public. Initially they were available from The Public Relations Officer, The Railway Executive, 222 Marylebone Road, and later from The Chief Publicity Officer, British Transport Commission, 363 Marylebone Road, the price remaining at 10 shillings throughout, from 1952 to 1960.

The absence of Nos 17 and 18 in the sequence is an unresolved question. Either these numbers were allocated to tests ultimately not made, or to tests made but for which it was difficult to reconcile the static, road test components, and the report was therefore rejected as unsatisfactory. There are candidate locomotives in both categories – pick your own! Further bulletins were "pencilled in" and concerned BR's growing fleet of main line diesels, but they would only have involved dynamometer cars and neither of the Rugby or Swindon plants.

Bulletin No 1 published May 1951

Modified "Hall" class 4-6-0 7916 *Mobberley Hall* built 1950

Static tests: Swindon test plant at speeds between 15 and 70mph.
Controlled road tests: Wantage Road-Filton with WR dynamometer car with loads of up to 550 tons and a maximum speed of 70mph. Indicator shelter also used when indicating cylinders.

The Engine had run 22,000 miles before being tested, plus 4,000 miles on the tests. Prior to these, some preliminary modifications were made to the blastpipe and chimney dimensions, producing appreciably higher steam rates of 22,000-23,000lb/hr. These alterations were subsequently applied to the rest of the class.

Bulletin No 2 published August 1951

B1 class 4-6-0 61353 (61B Ferryhill) built 1950

Static tests: Rugby testing station at steam rates up to 25,000lb/hr.
Controlled road tests: Carlisle-Skipton with LMR No 1 dynamometer car. Loads up to 436 tons, speeds up to 70mph.

The engine had run 46,000 miles from new before being prepared at Darlington Works for these tests, and a further 7,700 miles before the tests began. 3,150 miles were run at Rugby, and 1,950 miles on the road tests.

It had been originally intended that this loco should be tested with four exhaust systems, for comparison purposes. These were: single, plain double, Lemaitre multiple-jet and Kylchap double chimneys, and the smokebox was modified at Darlington so that each system could be quickly fitted. Unfortunately, pressure of time caused the cancellation of tests with the other systems, and all tests were carried out with the standard single chimney. The only modification carried out prior to testing was to rebalance the driving wheels to balance 70% of the reciprocating masses instead of the usual 30%.

Bulletin No 3 published October 1951

London Midland Region class 4 2-6-0 43094 built 1950

Static tests: Swindon test plant at speeds between 15 and 50mph.
Controlled road tests: Wantage Road-Filton with WR dynamometer car with loads up to 500 tons (passenger) and 1,000 tons (freight), indicator shelter used. Representative of a locomotive in somewhat less than first class condition.

As delivered to the test plant, this engine could only sustain 9,000lb steam per hour. Modifications were therefore made to the blastpipe and chimney dimensions and the ashpan air space, with the self-cleaning plates replaced by a spark-arrester netting. Together, these alterations lifted the maximum steam rate to 17,000lb/hr (an 89% improvement) and the engine was tested with these improvements in place, which were subsequently applied to the rest of the class.

Bulletin No 4 published January 1952

BR Standard class 4MT 4-6-0 75006 built 1951

Static tests: Swindon test plant at speeds between 15 and 50mph.
Controlled road tests: Didcot-Filton with WR dynamometer car, indicator shelter used. Representative of a loco in first class condition.

This engine had run only 4,600 miles from new, and ran 2,910 miles on test. No modifications were made to the locomotive, and a steam production rate of more than 19,000lb/hr was achieved on both the plant and on the road. On the road tests, 75006 handled up to 18 coaches (546 tons), and indicator records show that 1400 ihp was produced at 59mph at 31% cut-off, with a steam rate of 19,400lb/hr.

Bulletin No 5 published April 1953

BR Standard class 7MT 4-6-2 70005 *John Milton*
   built 1951 (first series)
BR Standard class 7MT 4-6-2 70025 *Western Star*
   built 1952 (second series)

Static tests: Rugby testing station – 70005: 6,890 miles,
   70025: 6,350 miles.
Controlled road tests: 70005 only, Carlisle-Skipton with
   LMR No 1 dynamometer car (and MTUs 2 and 3,
   Jan/Feb 1952 only), 5,000 miles covered on test.

As received at Rugby, 70005 had only run 560 miles from
new and 70025 only 1,040 miles. At full extent on the last
road test, and with two firemen, 70005 was able to raise
37,560lb steam/hr hauling 850 tons (20 coaches plus
dynamometer car and working MTUs) with a measured
horsepower of 2200-2300 at the drawbar. 70025 was tested
as a check on the results with 70005, with indicator diagrams
created by the "Farnboro" electric spark system.

Bulletin No 6 published May 1953

BR Standard class 5MT 73008 (63A Perth) built 1951

Static tests: Rugby testing station at speeds between 15 and
   75mph running 9,120 miles on the rollers.
Controlled road tests: Carlisle-Skipton with LMR No 1
   dynamometer car. 2,800 miles covered on the road.

73008 arrived at Rugby almost new, with only 800 miles "on
the clock". Preliminary runs brought about two modifications
– a different type of firebar was fitted that increased the air
space, and there was a small reduction in the blastpipe orifice,
which taken together raised the maximum steam production
rate by about 5,000lb/hr, these alterations being adopted for
the rest of the class. On the Ais Gill line, maximum effort
(with two firemen) produced 1530 drawbar hp with a 560 ton
load and a steam rate of 25,360lb/hr.

Bulletin No 7 published August 1953

War Department "Austerity" 2-8-0 90464 and 2-10-0 90772
   built 1940s

Controlled road tests (only): Carlisle-Hurlford with LMR
   No 3 dynamometer car and MTUs 1, 2 and 3. LMS
   corridor tender fitted behind both engines. 90464 was
   not tested above 40mph due to rough riding. Constant
   speed tests.

Both engines were given general repairs and then run-in for
500 miles before undergoing 3,500 miles (each) on test. The
only modification prior to the test runs was to decrease the
diameter of the blastpipe on both engines, which were
indicated by a "Farnboro" indicator in the dynamometer car.
A self-weighing grate was also used on these two engines.

Both engines were built with the same sizes of cylinders
and driving wheels and the same boiler pressure, so that their
calculated "tractive effort" is identical. However, the 2-10-0
had much the larger boiler and firegrate, and these two
factors, plus the better adhesion of the 5-axle engine, gave the
2-10-0 a marked superiority over the 2-8-0 in all respects. It
is therefore unfortunate that BR had over 700 of the 2-8-0s
and only 25 of the 2-10-0s, a far more competent and efficient
type.

Bulletin No 8 published March 1953

Eastern Region class V2 2-6-2 60845 (35A New England)
   built 1939

Static tests: Swindon test plant running 4,053 miles there and
   on the road in total.
Controlled road tests: Reading-Filton with WR dynamometer
   car and up to 762 tons behind the tender, indicator
   shelter used. Tests hampered by foggy weather. Engine
   driven by WR crew unfamiliar with Gresley 3-cylinder
   types.

The main purpose of these tests was to improve the engine's
steaming when fitted with self-cleaning plates, which had
caused significant deterioration in this capability. As
received at Swindon, only 14,000lb/hr could be raised
compared to 24,000lb/hr without the plates. The whole of the
exhaust arrangement within the smokebox was therefore
redesigned (chimney, petticoat and blastpipe), following
which (and with self-cleaning plates fitted) 30,000lb of steam
could be raised per hour – more than doubling the
evaporation rate! Indicator diagrams also revealed a
remarkable difference in the performance of the outside and
middle cylinders, though no modifications were made at
Swindon to correct this. All-out, 60845 registered 1870 ihp at
74½mph with a steam rate of 28,400lb/hr on a 25-coach load
(762 tons).

Bulletin No 9 published November 1952

Main line diesel electric 1750hp 1Co-Co1 10202 built 1951

Controlled road tests (only): 1pm Waterloo-Exeter (Central)
   and 7am Exeter-Waterloo service trains with WR
   dynamometer car. First series: June/July 1952 with gear
   ratio 52:21. Second series: October 1952 with gear ratio
   65:17. Test trains between Exeter (Central) and
   Salisbury.

The locomotive had run 89,270 miles prior to the service train
tests, received an intermediate overhaul (and gear ratio
change) at 100,880 miles, and had run 130,310 miles when
the second series commenced. The altered gear ratio was
beneficial below 20mph with little difference at higher
speeds. Maximum drawbar hp registered was 1300-1325, and
was deemed well suited to mixed traffic duties.

Bulletin No 10 published January 1954

<u>Southern Region class 8P 4-6-2 35022 *Holland America Line*</u>
built 1948

Static tests: Rugby testing station at speeds between 15 and
85mph. "Farnboro" indicator used.
Controlled road tests: Carlisle-Skipton with LMR No 1
dynamometer car. Maximum load 594 tons, (20-coach
train).

The engine received a classified repair 1,115 miles before
reaching Rugby. It then ran 10,300 miles on the rollers
followed by 3,840 miles on the road (March to November
1952). With a modified chimney and blastpipe arrangement,
a further 2,460 miles was run at Rugby (March to May 1953)
and an extra 2,820 miles at Rugby with a boiler with no
thermic syphon between December 1953 and January 1954.
Maximum power produced was 2485 ihp at 75mph. On the
test plant, it proved possible (with two firemen) to generate
42,000lb of steam per hour, but no higher rate could be
attempted due to chronic slipping at high power outputs. This
tendency was duplicated on the road tests as well, and full
regulator working was not possible at either location. The
valve motion proved to be erratic, and leakages of oil from
the oil-bath of the chain-driven valve gear caused the rollers
of the test plant to have to be wiped clean at intervals. The
engine was heavier on coal to the tune of 15-20% in
comparison with other engines of similar dimensions, and the
presence or absence of syphons had little effect.

Bulletin No 11 published April 1959

<u>English Electric 1000hp Type 1 diesel Bo-Bo D8000</u>
built 1957

Static load tests: Derby Works diesel test house.
Controlled road tests: Toton-Rugby-Toton with LMR No 3
dynamometer car and MTUs 1 and 2.

The locomotive had run 18,650 miles prior to testing, with a
further 2,240 miles on the road, from July to September 1958.
Tests included slow-speed running at 5 or 2½mph, and on 15
coaches (452 tons) plus dynamometer car over the route from
Toton to Derby, Chesterfield, Chapel-en-le-Frith, Ambergate
and back to Toton. Drawbar horsepower was 76.2% of
engine output and overall thermal efficiency was 24.2%. The
engine performed well with no significant electrical or
mechanical defects arising.

Bulletin No 12 published March 1960

<u>BTH/Paxman 800hp Type 1 diesel Bo-Bo D8208</u> built 1958

Static load tests: Derby Works diesel test house.
Controlled road tests: Route as for D8000 with LMR No 3
dynamometer car with MTUs 1 and 2. Also Toton-
Buxton-Toton and Toton-Edale-Toton.

This locomotive had a mileage of 5,900 before the road tests,
and covered 2,530 miles on them, which included haulage of
twenty 16-ton mineral wagons weighing 483 tons. The
locomotives were intended for transfer freight duties around
the north of London. (See photographs on pages 68 and 73.)
Preliminary tests showed that the diesel engine output
was seriously deficient due to the maladjustment of the
governor and power was also lacking at speeds in excess of
50mph. Both these electrical issues were corrected before the
tests began, and all locos of this class were similarly dealt
with. Drawbar horsepower was 620 (maximum) and the
working (in general) agreed with the manufacturer's ratings.

Bulletin No 13 published July 1959

<u>BR Standard class 9F 2-10-0s 92013 and 92050</u> built 1954
to 1955

Static tests: Rugby testing station at speeds between 15 and
55mph (60mph on the road).
Controlled road tests: 92013 Carlisle-Skipton with LMR
No 3 dynamometer car and MTUs 1, 2 and 3 and a load
of 25 16-ton mineral wagons (642 tons). Tests carried
out between September and October 1954. 92050
Carlisle-Hurlford between November and December
1955. Tests as for 92013.

Both engines had only run 500 to 1,000 miles from new,
followed by 2,500 to 4,000 miles at Rugby and a further
2,000 to 2,500 miles on the road. Both sustained 28,000 to
29,000lb/hr, at which rate 1915 ihp was being produced at
35mph and 42% cut off. The only modification was to
slightly reduce the blastpipe diameter. At 60mph the riding
of the engine was admirably smooth. Note the considerable
delay between the conclusion of the tests and the publication
of this Bulletin. This was due to discrepancies between the
Derby results (CRTs) and the Rugby results, and required a
further visit of 92050 to Rugby (in March/April 1957) to
reconcile the two.

Bulletin No 14 published circa March 1960

<u>Brush 1250hp Type 2 diesel A1A-A1A D5516</u> built 1958

Controlled road tests (only): Passenger service trains with ER
dynamometer car: 8.30am Liverpool Street-Norwich (7
stops) and 2.45pm Norwich-Liverpool Street (1 stop).
Freight trains with ER dynamometer car: 1.37pm
Temple Mills-Whitemoor (405 tons) and 8.36am
Whitemoor-Temple Mills (610 tons).

Special freight runs hauling 900-1,100 tons were also made
between Cambridge and Elsenham. The locomotive had run
16,700 miles at the end of the trials. Performance was
satisfactory and consistent with the maker's specifications.
Maximum horsepower at the drawbar was 982 at 20mph on
level track, making this type well suited to mixed traffic
duties. The locomotive was in good condition and there were

no mechanical or electrical faults of any consequence during the tests.

Bulletin No 15 published 1957

<u>BR Standard class 8P 4-6-2 71000 *Duke of Gloucester*</u>
   built 1954

Static tests: Swindon test plant at speeds up to 75mph.
Controlled road tests: Swindon-Reading-Westbury-Swindon with WR dynamometer car and test loads of 459 and 586 tons. Indicator shelter used.

This engine was fitted with British Caprotti rotary-cam poppet valves, and it was the behaviour of these valves that was of particular interest. The engine was run at up to 90mph on road tests, and at 75mph, 2500 ihp was produced at a steam rate of 32,000lb/hr and only 20% cut off, though the engine showed a healthy appetite for coal.

   The total mileage at Swindon and on the road was 7,450, and after initial attention to various oil feeds, no trouble was experienced. Interestingly, analysis of the test results showed that the most efficient working of this loco extended over a considerable range of heavier loadings and higher speeds, not at the lowest speeds nor with lighter loads. Train timings based on these results were also included in the Bulletin.

Bulletin No 16 published February 1956(?)

<u>Main line diesel electric 2000hp 1Co-Co1 10203</u> built 1954

Controlled road tests (only): Waterloo-Exeter with WR dynamometer car. First series: special trains with various loads, 63 to 392 tons. Second series: service trains, 1pm Waterloo-Exeter, 5.55pm return.

This engine had completed 106,000 miles, with no more than normal servicing, before these tests, at which the diesel engine efficiency at full load had fallen by 4% and power output by 3% from its maximum design performance. 10203 had, at 109.5 tons, 60% more adhesion weight than any British express passenger steam engine, and was fitted with an infinitely variable power control handle (instead of a series of predetermined notch positions as on 10202).

Bulletin No 19 published circa May 1958

<u>English Electric prototype 3300hp diesel Co-Co *Deltic*</u>

Controlled road tests (only): Carlisle-Skipton with LMR No 3 dynamometer car and MTUs 1, 2 and 3. (On two days the ER car was also used).

This locomotive had, by virtue of its compact design, two 1650hp 18-cylinder high-speed engines, and weighed only 106 tons – a world record power to weight ratio. Tests were carried out using one or both engines, and over 5,000 miles were covered on the Ais Gill route. Although two MTUs

were used for most of the tests, a 20-coach train of 642 tons was used for a Durran Hill-Hellifield round trip of 165 miles, covered at an average speed of 56.2mph. Overall fuel consumption was such that a return run from Euston to Glasgow, or King's Cross to Edinburgh was thought to be well within the locomotives 800 gallon fuel capacity. The Bulletin commented favourably on the smoothness of the riding and freedom from vibration, the only criticism being its noisiness when idling or standing in a station.

Bulletin No 20 published circa January 1960

<u>SR class 8P 4-6-2 35020 *Bibby Line*</u> rebuilt 1956

Controlled road tests (only): Exeter-Salisbury-Waterloo with WR dynamometer car. First series: special trains Exeter-Salisbury and back. Second series: service trains (with increased weights) using the 3pm Waterloo-Exeter and the 12.30pm up Atlantic Coast Express.

Engines of this class were all rebuilt at Eastleigh from 1956 to 1959 to eliminate the chain-driven valve gear immersed in an oil-bath that had given trouble in service and at Rugby Testing Station (Bulletin 10). Standard Walschaerts valve gear was therefore fitted and the air-smoothed casing removed, substantially altering their appearance. Boiler pressure was reduced from 280 to 250lb/sq in, a new ashpan was fitted and some changes were made to the draughting arrangements.

   On the heavier Waterloo trains (approximately 500 tons), the maximum performance recorded was on 28th June 1956, when 1500hp was measured at the drawbar when climbing Honiton bank.

Bulletin No 21 published December 1960

<u>BR/Sulzer Type 2 diesel 1160hp Bo-Bo D5008</u> built1959

Static load tests: Derby Works diesel test house.
Controlled road tests: Routes as for D8208 with LMR No 3 dynamometer car with MTUs 1 and 2. Constant speed test controlled by MTU. Also in service conditions on a 15-coach load with no MTUs.

The locomotive had covered 2,624 miles before the testing programme and 4,211 miles on it. All tests were carried out in a satisfactory manner, and performance was closely in accord with the maker's specification. One extra fitting was added during the course of the tests to improve the handling of the locomotive at a low controller settings and this became standard to the rest of the class.

Opposite: The cover of Bulletin 12, published in March 1960, and described on page 71. (Nick Wheat Collection)

Chapter 13

Observations

What then were the benefits of all the testing during this period? Is it possible to identify from the results particular changes in the practices of the time, or even specific improvements to rail services?

The majority of the testing carried out in these years was concerned with the steam locomotive, and it is clear that at least some benefits accrued. At the start of the BR era, the 1948 Interchange Trials, together with Swindon test plant's work on draughting arrangements within the smokebox, did assist in the production of almost 1000 new engines of standard types. These had wide route availability, were robust, simple to maintain, and suited to the tasks required of them. Much of Swindon's work in this early period was both fruitful and could be fitted cheaply. Higher superheat was tested and applied to major GWR passenger classes, and it was found that even minor alterations to the chimney and blastpipe dimensions dramatically increased the steaming capacity of a wide range of engine types.

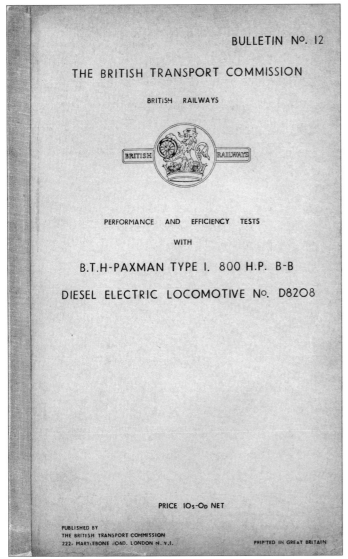

However after 1952/3, apart from some useful testing with double chimneys (largely on WR engines), the Swindon test plant's contribution declined, but with only one or two locos being tested per year in its latter years this is hardly surprising. Interestingly, during 1954, the plant was again modified, this time by the addition of hydraulic brakes to a fourth set of rollers. The reasoning behind this remains obscure however, as neither 8-coupled steam engines nor Bo-Bo diesels were subsequently tested here.

One positive result of the tests at Rugby was the eventual rebuilding of all the "Merchant Navy" class Pacifics to a more economical form, as well as many of the smaller but similar "West Country" and "Battle of Britain" classes. Disappointingly, none of the innovations trialled at Rugby found worthwhile application in a BR setting. Crosti boilers and mechanical stokers were fitted to some 9Fs but later removed as unnecessary complications, neither giving the economy expected. One of the last 9Fs was given a Giesl ejector as a trial, but with hindsight this useful device was not only fitted too late (1959) for wholesale adoption, but to the wrong engine for noticeable savings to be made.

When reviewing the list of LMS locomotives tested at Rugby, whilst the "Royal Scot" and the "Jubilee" were sent in an effort to improve their steaming, on what grounds the "Duchess" appeared is something of a mystery. Both 46165 and 45722 left the plant with improved steaming capabilities (though these modifications were not widely applied to the other class members) but 46225, as far as the author is aware, left with no modification whatsoever, either recommended or implemented!

Contrast all this effort with Doncaster's (slightly later, 1957/8/9) fitting of double Kylchap exhausts that transformed the performance of the A3s and A4s provided with it – quick, cheap and with no testing required! Swindon was also currently fitting double chimneys to "Castles" and "Kings" whenever they passed through works, as a matter of course. Rugby's purpose was indeed to test, not design, and yet 6 months were allocated to development work on the private-venture gas turbine, following which some 8½ months were spent investigating enhanced superheat, both surely blind alleys at this late (1957/8) stage?

It is of course arguable that the Rugby Testing Station simply came onto the scene too late to be a really effective tool in enhancing the performance of the steam locomotive. It should however have had the advantage of having a "clean sheet" in the sense that both it, and BR had come into being at much the same time and that Company loyalties did not need to be overcome. The two key figures were formerly LNER and GWR men, but other personnel had very mixed backgrounds. A close working relationship between BR (via the Locomotive Testing Committee) and Rugby might therefore have been anticipated, but this does not seem to have been the case in practise, especially as time went on.

It is probably a slight exaggeration to suggest that Derby Research Department, Rugby and Swindon were "at each other's throats", with the Locomotive Testing Committee a distant even a disinterested spectator, but these three testing branches seemed to be as "independent" as the pre-Nationalisation Companies ever were! Co-operation and feedback between them appears at best to have been minimal, with the Locomotive Testing Committee's role restricted to dictating the programme and accepting (and filing) the subsequent reports, without communicating either the resulting action taken, or the overall "plan" to these centres, which in turn did not effectively disseminate any information to their workforce. (It was certainly the case at Rugby that some staff, working late into the evening, resorted to illicitly examining recent correspondence in the office, to find out what was going on!) Meanwhile, the Eastern Region testing team at Darlington, quietly aloof and disconnected from this fray, simply got on with the job.

Looking back, and acknowledging that during the 1950s and early 1960s much of BR's large volume of freight was handled by 0-6-0 and 2-8-0 types, the big surprise is that only the WD 2-8-0 and 2-10-0 types were given any sort of "performance and efficiency test", and even these were confined to road tests. Prior to Rugby opening, the Railway Executive referred the following proposal to the CMEs for comment, as being (in their judgement) suitable work with which Rugby could commence operations:

"To ascertain optimum chimney and blast pipe proportions for Eastern Region class B1 and London Midland Region class 5 engines, including comparisons between single, double and multiple jet blast pipes,"

To which DR Carling added the suggestion that the tests should be extended to include those classes which contain the most numerous engines.

Had this suggestion been acted upon, it is quite possible that, with such large numbers of 0-6-0 and 2-8-0 freight classes coming under this "most numerous engine" category, considerable savings in coal and maintenance could have been achieved. The B1 was of course subsequently tested, though only with its single chimney, and some tests were carried out with a class 5, but quite why Carling's eminently sound suggestion was not vigorously pursued remains one of those disappointing aspects of Rugby's programme.

But the main thrust of all the steam locomotive testing was to establish the capacity and the limitations of the engines being tested, and hence the range of speeds and loads at which the locomotive could be economically worked. Some timetables were compiled with these specific properties in mind, but as the maximum power output of a steam engine was not achieved economically, duties requiring steam to be worked this hard would be allocated to a diesel or electric type whose characteristics suited full power working. Hence, the fastest, heaviest trains went over to diesel haulage fairly quickly, leaving steam traction restricted to mixed traffic or freight workings that were comfortably within its economic range.

Use of the dynamometer cars was extremely varied, and their high-profile employment in the controlled road tests – some of which became bulletins in the public domain – was but a small fraction of their work. As stated earlier, reports were written by the dynamometer car staff at the conclusion of each test and these were then submitted to the Locomotive Testing Committee for their analysis. Unfortunately few of these documents seem to have survived, or are not generally available and hence a detailed record of how tests were conducted, and the resulting recommendations, is not available. However, even the basic facts of where, when, for how long and with what locos the cars were in use is quite revealing.

Before consulting the dynamometer car logs, even the author was unaware of the vast majority of their contents, surprised by their diverse nature and their application to such a wide variety of railway equipment. Just how useful all these tests turned out to be in promoting any changes in the then current practices is of course unknown. The Locomotive Testing Committee passed on any recommendations it felt were justified to the BTC (or the BRB) after which its job was done, and what happened higher up the ladder was not their concern. However it would seem that in the final outcome, precious little of the testing effort (static or on the road) was found to be directly beneficial to BR. This was especially so after the announcement of the Modernisation Plan in 1955, as BR's rolling stock procurement programme was thereafter increasingly in the hands of private industry, particularly as regards locomotives.

Later work in testing non-steam types with dynamometer cars largely acted as confirmation of the manufacturer's specifications, together with some useful fault-finding work. At the end of the timescale considered here, with higher speeds becoming more common, greater attention was being paid to the riding of vehicles, their effect on the track, and to wheel/rail adhesion properties. These tests foreshadowed many of the procedures of the next decade, and in recognition of this, all testing staff and cars were concentrated at Derby from 1967, when the new Railway Technical Centre opened. It had taken nearly 20 years, but at long last BR had managed to centralise all its testing capabilities.